Divining
the primary
sense

Frontispiece: Lawrence J. Veale demonstrating the Revealer field detector

Divining the primary sense

Unfamiliar radiation in
nature, art and science

Herbert Weaver

With an Introduction by
Mike Weaver

Routledge & Kegan Paul
London, Henley and Boston

First published in 1978
by Routledge & Kegan Paul Ltd
39 Store Street,
London WC1E 7DD,
Broadway House,
Newtown Road,
Henley-on-Thames,
Oxon RG9 1EN and
9 Park Street,
Boston, Mass. 02108, USA
Set in Theme by
The Pentagon Printing Group
Soho Square, London W1
and printed in Great Britain by
Lowe & Brydone Ltd
Thetford, Norfolk

ISBN 0 7100 8734 9

To Boo

Contents

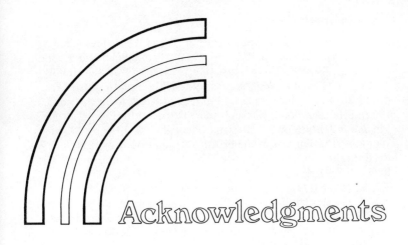

Acknowledgments

I would like to thank the following people who have helped me with some items in my research, but who should not be held responsible for my ideas and opinions: Ann Brock, James Chambers, W.A. Dawes, Captains Harry Harvey and Garth Halanen, David Mayor, Litz Pisk, R. Rosser, Captains R.N. Thompson and T.M. Tarrant of Trinity House. I am especially grateful to Alan Milward for making some experimental apparatus as requested; Paul Oliver for his kind interest; Mrs Elsie Veale for her warm encouragement over many years; and my family for their co-operation, tolerance and support. Chapter I is an attempt to repay the large debt I owe to Lawrence Veale, who opened a new gate into a long-forgotten physical world.

The author and publisher would like to thank the following for permission to reproduce illustrations: Devon News Services Ltd (frontispiece); Mme A. Laming-Emperaire (Fig 2.1, after A. Laming, *Lascaux*, 1959); Hutchinson Publishing Group and Curtis Brown Ltd (Figs 2.2, 3.11 (adapted), from J.G.D. Clark and S. Piggott, *Prehistoric Societies*, 1965); Basic Books Ltd (Fig. 2.5, after C. Gordon, *Forgotten Scripts*, 1968); Routledge & Kegan Paul Ltd (Fig. 2.6, from Sir E. Wallis Budge, *The Egyptian Language*, 1966); W.K. Martin (Fig. 2.7, from W.K. Martin, *The Concise British Flora in Colour*, Photocopyright George Rainbird Ltd, 1965); Hamish Hamilton Ltd (Fig. 3.2, after R.J.C. Atkinson, *Stonehenge* Copyright © 1955 R.J.C. Atkinson, Hamish Hamilton, London); Thames & Hudson Ltd (Figs 3.3, 3.9 (adapted), from P. Rawson, *Art of South-East Asia*, 1967; Fig. 3.14, after W. Watson, *Early Civilization in China*, 1966; Fig. 4.3, from M.E.L. Mallowan, *Early Mesopotamia and Iran*, 1965); Paul Oliver

Acknowledgements

(Fig. 3.6, after *Shelter and Society*, ed. P. Oliver, 1971; Figs 3.7, 3.8, after *Shelter in Africa* ed. P. Oliver, 1970); Picture Point Ltd, London (Fig. 3.12); Asia Publishing House (Fig. 3.15, from R.A. Jairazbhoy, *An Outline of Islamic Architecture*, 1972); Princeton University Press (Fig. 3.16, after J. Finnegan, *Archaeology of World Religions*, vol.3, 1952); Schocken Books Inc. and Andre Deutsch Ltd (Fig. 4.1, from *Voodoo in Haiti* by Alfred Metraux Copyright © 1959 by Alfred Metraux); The Trustees of the British Museum (Fig. 4.2); A.H. & A.W. Reed (Fig. 4.4, from R. Robinson, *The Australian Aboriginal*, 1968); Routledge & Kegan Paul Ltd and Princeton University Press (Figs 4.6, 5.2, 5.5, from C.G. Jung, *Psychology and Alchemy*, Collected Works, vol.12, 1968); Litz Pisk (Fig. 4.7); The British Library Board (Fig. 5.3, from Royal MS. 6 EVI, f.535v.); Robert Harding Associates, London (Fig. 5.4); John Wiley & Sons (Fig. 5.6, from W.W. Robbins, T.E. Weier and C.R. Stocking, *Botany: An Introduction to Plant Science*, 1966); Mme Lacouture (Fig. 4.5).

Introduction

Imagine a water-diviner interested in most things except
water, and you can place my father's work roughly already.
You may assume that it must, then, be minerals; and you are
right about one thing — my father first met the inventor of
the apparatus that he uses when Lawrence Veale came to
Cornwall in search of tin for a small company in which they
both had a few shares. Divining-rods were used for mining
in the Middle Ages at least a hundred years before they were
used to find water, and were first introduced to Britain in
Cornish mines.[1]

But it would not do to think of my father as a metal-
diviner, because he is no longer much concerned with
minerals. For the last seven years he has been following up
the implications of two basic discoveries made by Lawrence
Veale. One discovery was that the instrument can be adapted
to respond to organic as well as inorganic matter, and so
sensitively that it can match one half of a leaf of grass to its
other half. The other discovery was that to interpose a simple
sign (like a cross drawn roughly on paper) between the
instrument and the half-leaf of grass is to impede the
instrument's response. In other words, Veale discovered that
he could detect unique signals in organic matter and that
certain configurations could cause their suppression. From
this my father has evolved a theory of the use of signs in art

and nature. The individuality of human beings, as well as of grass plants, is a physical reality. If these discoveries were developed for saving the lives of missing persons it would obviously benefit mankind. Unfortunately, in the hands of an enemy of whatever kind, nobody without a defensive sign-system would be safe from such a method of detection.

No doubt claims like this have been made before and have turned out to be fraudulent. In America divining is called 'witching', and its whole history is bedevilled, literally, by association with witchcraft. The common English name for it is 'dowsing', but nobody has noticed that John Locke when he used the word in its first recorded form spelled it 'Deusing'.[2] Martin Luther thought that to practise it broke the first commandment.[3] What the deuce (or devil) next! It has been suggested, often, that in the seventeenth century the scientific imagination began to separate from the artistic and religious imagination; the facts of chemistry began to displace the imagery of alchemy, for instance. My father, whom I remember in my youth as an anti-clerical rationalist, who happened (somewhat inconsistently, it seemed at the time) to be also interested in Freud and Jung, now regards the scientific establishment as unimaginative and the religious establishment as at least acknowledging the dynamic energy of the cosmos, even when busily deadening its influence with suppressive forms. He sees modern man as an Ishmael cast out of the paradise which allowed him to respond to all other organisms by means of his 'primary' sense, and which others, perhaps mistakenly, call the sixth sense or extra-sensory perception. He maintains an anti-psychical interpretation of parascience consistent with his rationalism, believing that the primary sense, which Veale's instrument amplifies, is a concrete and measurable means of understanding what art and religion objectify in imagery and symbolism. Today, the scientific establishment is recognizing that these claims should be verified: 'Now surely is the time for scientists in large numbers to take a more practical interest in these obstinate issues. If we fail to do so, parascience will recede further into the mystic's world and will take with it much of the public's sympathy.'[4]

What is this instrument that has largely taken the place of

the forked twig of the traditional diviner in the civil engineering field? It consists of a pair of chromium-plated handles with rods mounted in them on ball-bearings, and turned at right angles where they emerge from the handles. These handles enclose aerial systems tuned to respond to specific minerals. In the starting position the operator holds the rods parallel; for the beginner this is less difficult than trying to ride a bicycle for the first time. When the operator moves over an objective the rods may cross over each other, or open outwards. From these basic movements the operator can interpret what it is he has found, sometimes using additional apparatus. How the Revealer functions is not known, although various explanations exist for the working of such instruments of which this is perhaps the most effective to date. The 'power' used comes from the operator himself, not from any external source.

Broadly speaking, there are psychical and physical theories to explain the working of such 'autoscopes'. The dominant one is that propounded by Barrett and Besterman. This is a psychical theory of 'unconscious muscular action', or what Faraday called *quasi* involuntary action'; but whereas Faraday rejected its significance out of hand, Barrett and Besterman were persuaded that the dowser has some unknown capacity for second sight.[5] This theory depends partly on psychokinesis — the ability to make objects move consciously or unconsciously. On the contrary, my father believes that the main mental factor in 'Revealing' should be *anti*-psychokinetic in order to prevent any conscious or unconscious adjustment of the rods which impedes their natural movement. Anxiety, nervousness, or other forms of excitation can also inhibit the action of the rods. His own theory is a physical one which rests on the idea that there is a latent sensory faculty shared by all of us, which is likely to be explained eventually by biophysics, and applied for the benefit of mankind (and perhaps to its cost) by bionics.

S.W. Tromp, the most scientific investigator of the dowsing phenomenon, makes a distinction between unconscious muscular response to psychic processes and physiological response in the shoulder muscles to physical forces.[6] My father takes the physiological view. Lyall Watson offers the following summary:[7]

The sum total of hard knowledge about dowsing seems to amount to this: Water, by the action of friction between itself and the soil, creates a field that could have electromagnetic properties. Rubber and leather insulate this field, but metals seems to have no effect. Metals themselves, perhaps by their position in the earth's magnetic field, also exert a field effect. The fields created or modified by inorganic objects are appreciable to some animals and people. An unconscious sensitivity to these fields can be made manifest by using an object such as a rod or a pendulum as a visible indicator of field strength and direction.

Field-perception results, perhaps, from interaction between the life-field of the dowser and geophysical fields in the external world. My father's work extends this interaction to biological fields. However, according to H.S. Burr's dynamic field theory: 'The field both determines and is determined by the particle.'[8] This means that there is already interplay between the separate fields and the matter contained within them. Thus, if man's whole body is a sensorium responsive to whole fields in nature, and all these fields are constantly variable, the dowser can maintain the micro-communication system only by a process of continuous adjustment to field conditions.

My father believes that man has given up his birthright of the primary sense and encased himself in an armour of devices suppressive of contact with other organisms. He is more concerned with ecology than with the occult, and sees man's self-exclusion from interaction with the biological world as punitive. He would admit, however, that what is suppressive is also protective for man in his fallen state. I am rather less pessimistic. Over millenia, human nature does change, and with the help of an instrument like the Revealer new processes of thought and feeling more responsive to the surrounding universe may develop in man. Eventually, it might be possible for man to re-integrate his artistic, religious and scientific sensibilities in a unified imaginative faculty. My father's efforts tend in this direction.

Mike Weaver

1 Primary perception in living creatures

1 Lawrence Veale and the Revealer

This book was written from data collected while using the Revealer field detector which was invented and patented by the late Lawrence J. Veale, a retired building contractor who lived in Devonshire. Veale has paved the way, with a simple and practical device designed for use in civil engineering, for the investigation of mankind's most ancient but discarded endowment — the sensorial ability to detect distant elements and chemicals. In 1968 Veale told me that more than a thousand of his instruments had been sold, many of them overseas.

This field detector depends solely for its motive force on the waves, or particle emissions, issuing from the operator's body. The impulses are compressed and 'beamed' forward by the highly polished inner and lower surfaces of the chromium-plated instrument. The human-powered vectors originate in the vertebrae and issue from the general area of the thorax. This statement can be verified and demonstrated with a 'paramagnetic suppressor', the Revealer's equivalent of a ferromagnetic insulator. A suppressive or insulating badge — a metal cruciform — is a standard part of the Revealer equipment and it is worn on the operator's coat lapel to prevent signals from overhead chemical matter resonating with his projected beam during surface or underground detection. The instrument's reactions to the received signals begin as soon as you approach within 1·25 metres of the object or deposit. The edges of cuts made in the subsoil can also be detected with this instrument.

Veale was unable to detect water with a diviner's wand but wished to avoid the expense and inconvenience which underground problems can cause in building. He knew that some hypersensitive people can occasionally find buried objects using two pieces of bent wire. A regular system of amplifying and identifying signals received from the oscillations set up around objects of specific composition was essential to any successful apparatus designed to assist people who are not naturally responsive to such radiation. An enforced stay in hospital gave Veale the time he needed to work out some basic principles. In constructing his prototype Revealer by trial and error, he showed great patience and determination. It took him nearly three months to arrive at the measurements of the particular 'aerial spine' which would resonate only with salt-glaze sewer-pipe material. This entailed dismantling the apparatus for each length-reducing stroke of the file and re-assembling the instrument to test each time. The aerial spines are arranged in three tiers and mounted within the protection of the handles.

The Revealer's considerable commercial success in the field of civil engineering owes much to the length of underground targets such as trenches for sewer pipes and electric and other services. Wherever such a line is crossed, instrumental reaction occurs. The plastic insulation over a wire can also be detected as ferromagnetic insulators have no inhibiting effects within the frequencies used by the Revealer. Another factor in Veale's commercial success with the instrument lay in the eminently practical attitudes of the building trade in which he worked. His associates were able simply to practise handling the instrument over a visible target, test it in a likely area and, after confirming the results by digging, buy it. Veale and his chief demonstrator, Mr Walker, were exceptionally accurate in using the instrument in applications far beyond its original scope of finding the vertical position, depth and diameter and composition of a buried pipe.

Most people can learn to use the Revealer for its intended purpose, but for those of us who cannot match the practised accuracy of Veale and Walker a supplementary device now makes it possible to pin-point the exact vertical position of wires, pipes and mineral deposits. Similarly the precise position of the void edges or sides of underground chambers, fissures or mine-workings of whatever age can be determined by this addition.

It was, however, Lawrence Veale's parlour tricks, with which he amused his friends, which led to my most important developments of the Revealer's use. I watched Veale demonstrating how a grass leaf would only produce the instrumental response when he approached its parent plant among countless thousands on a lawn. This disclosed the fact that a unique, personal signal is emitted by each individual specimen in fauna and in flora except where the roots or bulbs of a plant have been split to make another plant which then shares the original's individuality. George de la Warr had already used the radiational links between an organism, its blood and its photograph in radiaesthetic treatments.[1]

During my association with Lawrence Veale, I, using a new technique which concentrated all the operator's energy output on to either aerial system as desired, disclosed and identified ray-paths or particle-streams linking an individual organism uniquely to its dispersed bodily portions over immense distances, and apparently by ionospheric reflection as with radio signals. It is the unique characteristic of an organism's personal signal which makes such identification possible. The rays which link deposits of identical inorganic chemical composition may also be used over strictly controlled and limited distances; experiments show that a photograph contains not only the reflected light rays of the subject but also both the unique personal signal and a blueprint of the chemical state of health at the time of photographic exposure. This information is continually re-broadcast from the photograph. Similarly, a voice-recording on magnetic tape is linked with the owner and can also be used in obtaining his or her general direction. My prototype apparatus and techniques for the directional location of missing persons, using a personal bodily item such as hair, blood sample or a photograph as a radiational matcher, is outlined in section 3 of this chapter.

These original experiments were conducted by Veale and myself in Penzance during 1967. The interception of a bird's flight-path, using one of its feathers and my artificial ray-linking device, showed the creature's shifts in direction which affected the position of the rods of the Revealer. This led to further experiments and to my theory concerning the puzzle posed by homing-efficiency in returning migrants, and co-operation between plant- and animal-life in the long-distance advertisement and location of food. The scientific and technical extension of these discoveries will lie in the successful determination of the fundamental frequencies within which this system works, and the conversion of the received electrically charged responses of the operator's body to oscilloscope scrutiny or sonic monitoring. Success in this development will lead to a completely foolproof and more easily worked distance-detection system.

The momentous discovery of the paramagnetic suppressor, which controls the chemical interchange phenomenon in nature, was accidental. Lawrence Veale told me about one occasion when he was invited to locate some valuable buried cables. These had been ploughed into a field for safe keeping during the Second World War. When peace came their exact location had been forgotten. The first signals which Veale received during his Revealer search proved to be misleading — digging produced nothing. A similar error occurred at another place close by. Nevertheless, Veale knew that he was certainly receiving metallic radiations. Faced with this problem he fiddled absent-mindedly with two paper-clips attached separately to the lapel of his jacket. He must have aligned them in some special configuration for when he checked the same places again the signals had disappeared. Glancing upwards he noticed that a very high wire crossed the site. It was the metallic signals from this that he had been receiving. A short series of paper-clip crossings and separations confirmed beyond doubt the capacity of this configuration to shield him from radiational interference from above. On a later occasion he was to find that two cross-brooches, one attached to each of his trouser turn-ups, blocked the reception of metal or mineral emissions from below them, while leaving him open to receive signals from above after he had removed his lapel cross.

After a loss over many millenia, a working understanding of the physical force-fields extending from certain signs — prehistoric man's outstanding scientific discovery — had been accidentally restored to modern man. It seems almost banal to add that Veale soon found his cables. Their ends were traced with the Revealer and attached to a tractor which pulled them out of the soft earth as a blackbird extracts a worm from the ground, having located it by similar means.

Veale first showed me his similar carbon-sign demonstration in Penzance in 1967. On clean paper he drew, separately, signs which he showed to be radiating their carbon content and contrasted them with other signs which suppressed not only their own carbon emissions but also the former emissions of material which had now been placed beneath those suppressive force-fields. It is the very form or shape of a suppressive sign which spreads a paramagnetic screen around itself and provides an impenetrable barrier to chemical interchange within the frequencies on which the Revealer operates. Veale then drew a nearly completed circle, leaving the circumference open by about one-eight of an inch. This figure signalled its carbon content. Then he completed the circle accurately, and the signals ceased. By adding a minute, external tail to the circle without cutting across its circumference the carbon signals were released to produce a response. Next he drew one graphite-pencil line which signalled its carbon. This he cut by another carbon line, producing a four-limbed cross. The cross did not signal. A six-limbed cross signalled; an eight-limbed one did not, nor did twelve-, sixteen-, or other multiples of four-limbed crosses signal. Veale then asked if I would like to see more of this curiosity of four: I could hardly wait. Again, on fresh paper, Veale made one pencilled dot which signalled. Two dots and three dots signalled, but four would not. And so it went on with all dots added in line and all signalling except when a multiple of four had accummulated. 'It is a pattern of four', said the practical builder Veale, 'which stops the metal of the nails in the floorboards of houses from vibrating when

5

the planks are properly laid. You see, when the carpenter secures the boards, end-to-end, he knocks in only four nails, two at the end of each meeting plank.' Thus Veale casually disclosed the secret of the protective physical essence lodged in the sacred tetraktys, the quaternary numerical dominant which has occupied the minds of scientific philosophers from Pythagoras to Jung.

2 The hypothetical existence of the primary sense

My own amateur experiments rest on the following hypothesis: Deposits of identical chemical matter, separated by distance, are radiationally linked on their precise frequency unless interrupted through the interpolation of force-fields of suppressive sign-forms. The suppressor must be formed from a homogeneous substance.

The crucial importance of four-units and their multiples in suppressing or containing chemical radiation seems to find a common basis in atomic chemistry. J.A.R. Newlands, during his work on comparative atomic weights, found, among other things, that the elements 4, 12, and 20 — separated by eight places from each other — closely resembled each other in melting-points, density and hardness. Commenting on this Louis Vaczek says: [2]

> We must conclude that having 8 electrons outermost seems to produce an extremely stable atom. That outer shell of 8, which all the rare gases have, cannot be broken . . . in the inert gases the energy distribution is so perfectly balanced that almost nothing chemical can disturb it. An atom with 8 electrons outermost is almost free of inner tensions, as it were.

The lack of inner tensions in an atom guarded by eight electrons is a perfect simile for four-multiple mandala reassurance.[3]

Concerning pheromones, substances influencing other members of the same animal species, Edward O. Wilson writes, 'It is becoming increasingly clear, however, that chemical systems provide the dominant means of communication in many animal species, perhaps even in most.'[4] Veale made his original discovery that a person's saliva, deposited on tissue-paper, could be individually checked for biochemical tissue-salts with the Revealer. This detection was limited to within 1·25 metres distance from the deposit. Since I was able to extend the range of the instrument's detection capability, the resonant interflow of chemicals between widely separated people is easily demonstrated by a new method. Two people are seated in chairs facing each other and separated by a distance of not less than 4 metres. Their chair-backs are then suppressed by two large crosses of bamboo sticks. This is to prevent any possible like-chemical signals (issuing from other organisms beyond the walls) intruding into the tests. The object is to test the joining ray which links the two people with each specific chemical that both enjoy. The operator takes two paces forward along the ray and a V-shaped displacement of the antennae rods occurs unless one or both of the subjects are deficient in that applied item. In that case the rods remain in the original parallel position and each person is then tested separately. The twelve tissue-salts used in these tests are calcium fluoride, calcium phosphate, calcium sulphate, ferrum phosphate, potassium chloride, potassium phosphate, potassium sulphate, magnesium phosphate, sodium phosphate, sodium sulphate, sodium chloride and silicic oxide.[5]

From tissue-salt checks made on many interested friends and acquaintances it seems that a surprisingly large number of people suffer a deficiency of one salt or another, often for long periods. While the resilience of the body may allow adjustments to such deficiencies to a certain extent, it is better when such deficiencies are absent — a twelve-cylinder engine will run more smoothly and trouble-free when all cylinders are firing evenly. One tested person told me that the disclosed deficiency, sodium phosphate, had been confirmed as deficient through an orthodox chemical analysis. However, another tested person — tested via his photograph — whom I found to be deficient in ferrum phosphate and potassium phosphate, was told that orthodox analyses could not be done with soluble compounds 'owing to the dissociation into ions in the body'. If this is so, then the radiational method described above, could open up a new field for useful chemical checks. When testing people in this way it is essential that the operator is broadcasting all the test items, otherwise the lack of resonance or signal response might be due to his own deficiency. A new Revealer technique has been found for tests on chemical compounds not naturally broadcast by the human body. This technique increases the scope beyond homoeopathic chemical checks and opens up possibilities concerning forensic and security applications.

A person's photograph provides a blueprint of his or her chemical state at the time of silver-halide film exposure. When testing the photographs of five individuals, each cut from a larger wedding group, it was found that all, resident and working in the area, were deficient in magnesium phosphate. However, the photographs of the best man and one bridesmaid were radiating that item — they were visitors to the area just for the wedding. During a return visit to the locality an opportunity offered itself for testing the same five local people in the flesh. The magnesium phosphate deficiency persisted. A sample of the corporation water was also deficient in that item. Another resident in the town who was tested on that occasion was found to be radiating strongly on magnesium phosphate. This seemed to demolish the area deficiency presumption until his wife remarked, 'but Jimmy goes to London every [working] day'. There, no doubt, Jimmy repaired his local deprivation of magnesium phosphate. When testing one person at a time, I habitually used my dog as one base-station to produce the biochemical rays with the human subject. Since moving to this town for permanent residence even the dog suffers this particular deficiency and seems unable to renew it by the natural canine, grass-biting means.

A detailed theory, concerning the chemical controls of migration and of homing accuracy, emerges from the *prima facie* data obtained from the tests with the tissue-salts that had showed discrimination to be at molecular level, and from the other tests which demonstrated the operator's ability to 'home' along the ray-path joining him to his own dispersed bodily samples such as blood and hair, and a photograph.

A brief comparison of the distribution of the tissue-salt

biochemicals detected in organisms of different genera and species is given in Table 1.1. This suggests further chemical affinities among the food-hunting species and their prey and fodder groups, which would extend to their protein content. In Table 1.1 it is only the *absence* of a response to any of the twelve specific items that is listed, and it is presumed that the individual specimens were in normal health or condition. Thus the results would not represent deficiencies in any species but their normal tissue-salt endowments which are less than the mammalian complement of twelve.

TABLE 1.1

Tested subject	Items which were not signalling											
	1	2	3	4	5	6	7	8	9	10	11	12
Two separate pigeon feathers										10		12
Two different sea-gull feathers							7			10		12
Two mackerel							7			10		12
Two herrings							7			10		12
One dover sole							7			10		
One turbot							7					12
Seaweeds (*Fucus serratus, Laminaria saccharina*)							7			10		
Mussel, limpet and sea-snail		2				6	7				11	
Two large-white butterflies						6			9			
One small-white butterfly		2		4					9			
Brussels sprouts						6			9			
One ten-week cabbage				4		6			9			
Aphis on Brussels sprouts								8	9			
Bluebottle fly	(This fly was signalling all twelve)											

Key

1 calcium fluoride
2 calcium phosphate
3 calcium sulphate
4 ferrum phosphate
5 potassium chloride
6 potassium phosphate

7 potassium sulphate
8 magnesium phosphate
9 sodium chloride
10 sodium phosphate
11 sodium sulphate
12 silicic oxide

It will be seen that sea-gulls, mackerel and herrings enjoy those same nine items which did respond, and that Brussels sprouts share the same ten which the large-white butterflies also signalled. Sea organisms lack potassium sulphate and the

Brassicas and their dependants lack sodium chloride.

Others, beside Edward Wilson quoted above, have suspected the existence of a chemical communication system in nature. Georges Lakhovsky was prescient when he wrote: 'It seems more and more evident that the sense of direction originates from special radiations of ultra-short wavelength, emitted by the birds and insects themselves.'[6] It is into just such a world of micro-communication that the instructed Revealer user can now hesitantly enter.

The vibratory chemical interchange produces an automatic reflex response in creatures when the impulses stimulate certain parts of their bodies. Rays link all dispersed deposits of identical chemicals, on the ground or in other creatures, through resonance. Each chemical element or chemical compound is apparently being oscillated and thus radiates the pattern of its individual atomic arrangement. The food-seeking animal contains chemicals, both endemic and renewed by ingestion, which enable it to respond in resonance when it crosses a ray-path connecting a new, more intensely radiating food supply with its present, chemically waning feeding ground. The hunting animal thus senses and is able to follow the new food direction — along the ray-path joining the two pasturages — far beyond the distance limits of scent particles and sight.

The other vital chemical-resonance factor, which controls the accuracy of return flights to the original breeding place in the home country, is the uniquely personal signal allotted solely to each individual creature or plant. This seems to be of the opposite polarity to the one used in food-seeking vector projections. While the general chemical signals seem to travel at radio or electron speed, the personal signals have a vastly slower speed as it takes approximately 30 seconds for them to achieve circumambience of the globe via ionospheric reflection. It is this much slower speed of the personal signals which is the crucial determinant of the shorter route over the great-circle course which the creature must follow when homing. As the slow personal signal completes the resonance link very much earlier over the short, direct route it is this first received signal which is used by the homing creature and which gives it the direction.

3 Human simulation of the homing faculty in migratory animals

Whether man's loss of the use of the primary reflex-sense used by animals caused his immense intellectual expansion as compensation for that loss, or whether that new and untrustworthy instrument, intelligence, beguiled him into the neglect of the natural communication system, is academic. He has been forced to construct, over the centuries, successful if complicated hunting and navigational systems which, however brilliant they seem to us, are ponderous in their production and use when compared with the casual accuracy with which other creatures use the chemical-resonance system for hunting, navigation and homing.

An experimental method for testing the theory is this:
(a)   From a dead bird two feathers are removed. The body and one feather are placed on the ground about 4·5 metres apart. The second feather (surrogate for the flying bird) is held against the left-hand aerial system throughout the experiment. Starting from at least 2 metres away, to enable time for the resonance to build up in the aerial system, the bird is approached with the Revealer antennae rods balanced parallel to the ground. When about 1·25 metres away they begin to react to the pull of the bird's body and drift inwards to culminate in a cross-over above it. The same result is obtained when approaching and when over the feather Figure 1.1 (a).
(b)   To disclose the personal ray-link between the bird's body and the feather at the other terminus a new, concentrating method is used. Having approached a direct line between the bird and feather, at right angles to it (1), the rods drift inwards (2) until the crossing occurs directly over the ray (3). Re-setting the rods the operator turns his back on the feather and walks along the ray-path towards the bird's body. The rods immediately adopt a V-shaped equal displacement (4) until, within about 1·25 metres from that terminus, the inwards drift again occurs, with cross-over attaining when above the bird's body. The same effect occurs if the ray-path is followed from bird's body to feather.
(c)   If the flying bird (operator) drifts sideways off the ray-

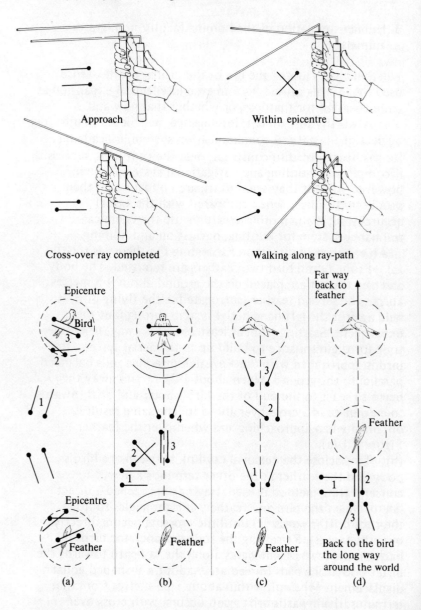

Approach

Within epicentre

Cross-over ray completed

Walking along ray-path

Figure 1.1 Bird to feather matching, local and distant

path centre the nearer antenna rod (wing) to that ray-path centre, which joins one station to the other, receives an inwards pull indicating the correction the bird must make to regain the centre line (2). The polarity of the operator is bestowed on the aerials of the instrument through his hands: accordingly birds appear to have positive polarity on the starboard wing and negative polarity on the port one.

(d)   To show the time-lag elapsing before the personal link becomes established the opposite way around the world, also on the same great-circle projection, an assistant first removes the bird's body and then the feather to a new site, allowing walking space beyond the feather of about 3 metres. Immediately the feather is placed the operator walks forwards and backwards at a right angle over a line extended from the bird through the feather and beyond it (1). After about 30 seconds the first quiver of the rods is followed by the completed cross-over above the extended line's centre (2). Turning away from that feather terminus and re-setting the rods the operator walks away from it along the extended line. Now the V-shaped displacement of the rods indicates the ray-path leading back to the bird's body via the long way around the world (3).

As the relatively slow travelling speed of personal emissions enables the signals of the shorter, direct route to be the first ones received, it would be folly to suppose that nature delays the 'wrong-way' links other than for this practical function.

Even from the scanty data obtained so far, a chemical sharing principle linking a creature to its related food and pollen plants emerges. It is not, of course, restricted to that biochemical tissue-salt range. The vibrant tone or signal level indicating a pasturage's chemical waxing period would be compared by the creatures with the current waning pasture when they crossed the rays linking both on the chemical frequencies in which they are interested. It is this change of signal intensity which compels the outward-bound migration flights to new feeding grounds.

The radiating pasturage target is a relatively wide one which even the novice first-flighter can scarcely miss, even when not guided by veterans (which appears to be the rule).The veteran, having visited that distant country before, can return

13

to an exact area that it had formerly found to be particularly attractive and where it had previously left its personal marker, such as a shed feather. The down, which signals at the base of a shed feather's vanes. protrudes in several directions and thus avoids the suppressive planes of the feather. Feather-down on the outside of a nest, or egg-shell fragments near to a nest, can be used as near-permanent homing targets for their bird owners. The egg-shell belongs to the hen and not to the chick that was in it. Although the plumes of a feather may succumb to fungi, the more impervious quills have a very long radiational life. Single feathers do not easily blow far away and the bird which sheds one knows enough not to leave it in a vegetation-suppressed situation.

Many bird species migrate in colony flights and prepare by prior assembly at departure points. The basis of the control system appears to be as follows. The lateral limits of the distant food 'fronts' are determined by the physical spread of insects and food plants within them, all coming to a seasonal radiational peak of intensity. So the target area may seem to us as very small at a distance of, say, 3,000 kilometres. However, there is only one centre line in a ray-path joining a veteran bird to its own feather left in the distant country. The bird colony has moved to the departure point well away from the breeding area where the personal deposits have already linked both ways around the world on the same great-circle projection. By excreting on 'take-off' and circling around that fresh deposit, veterans can easily find the shorter direction when it resonates with the distant marker-feathers. The birds are also attuned to the radiating quality of the food plantations in the same area. The width of the target food 'fronts' gives the novices in the flight many usable radiation bands within those lateral limits and enables them to keep station with the veterans at night.

The protective and aerodynamic considerations of V-formation squadrons and a leader's relief by other veterans during the flight must be observed. Where the colony's migration target area is as compact as its home one, each change of veteran leader enables that relief bird to home on its own previously shed feather target with a minimum of directional adjustment for the other flight members. It seems most likely that the position of each veteran in the flight formation is automatically determined by his personal feather's position at the far end, and that stations are only open to first-flighters on this understanding.

At the end of the migration season the target becomes the actual breeding area in the home country to which the birds will return. As the shorter route must again be determined, the assembly-point drill, away from the migration, feeding and roosting grounds, would be repeated; that is, initial direction-finding by veterans' excretions on take-off. The brief radiational life of excrement is, therefore, intended. While it can radiate for many days during dry weather the onset of heavy rain quickly leaches away its signalling capacity. This short radiational life prevents multiplication of distracting personal targets when the homing flight on to the stable feather (or egg-shell) base commences. Because of some risk that the initial excrement base-station might be destroyed by rain during the flight it seems important that a homing bird can revert to a more stable base-station, such as a feather left behind, as soon as is possible. As the distance between the take-off point and the roosting place would not be excessive, the subtended angle between the excrement base and the roosting-place feather would be very narrow and the ray-path based on the latter would soon merge during the flight.

Further experiments have shown the great importance of an animal's tail, which can act as a portable base-station. It is a chemically controlled 'rudder', so to speak, which enables the creature to make corrections to recover the permanent ray-link when diverted by gusts of wind or when avoiding predators. Squirrels raise the tail and spread its antennae-like hair when locating buried nuts which are then instantly found, and seized, by the apprehended chemical resonance, and not by scent. A dog's tail, when raised in the 'pointing' position, appears to act also as the base-station, thus completing the two-station resonance with the quarry's like-chemical emissions. To test these suppositions I fixed an artificial 'tail device' in the back of a jacket, in a position behind my vector-projecting area. Having found the direction of an organism, by crossing the line between it and its sample placed on the ground, that sample was then removed. The artificial tail enabled the established route to be followed, with the instrument displaying the V-form of the antennae rods, without the need of a fixed base-station.

Homing birds can make use of any vertical levels directly within the ray-paths which control the accuracy of their flights. When meeting physical obstacles directly in their ray-paths they are forced to go up-and-over, being submissive to the centralizing pull of the hairline thinness of the personal link. Should a bird land on a ship or on shore, either for a rest or because it has been blown widely off course, it can excrete on take-off and can soon find its permanent target's direction once more. Even if a ship, carrying a temporary base of excrement, continues on an oblique course the bird adjusts by keeping within the ray-link, pivoting around the 'hub' of the distant target. Similarly the Coriolis effect does not impede accurate contact with the flight-path, which is chemically controlled. The bird in transit, simply by maintaining resonance with its ray, automatically adjusts to the earth's eastward spin with its different surface-turning speeds at poles and equator.

A good example of homing on discarded egg-shells is afforded by the Green Turtle which breeds on Ascension Island in the South Atlantic. Duff Hart-Davis reports their homing accuracy when they return after a sojourn in Brazil lasting two or three years: 'They navigate 1,400 miles to a dot of land only seven miles wide, and even come back to the very beach on which they nested before.'[7] It is the discarded, enduring and leather-like egg-shells, left after the young have hatched above tide-level in the sand pit in which they were laid, on which the female turtle 'owner' unerringly homes. She is controlled over the whole swim by keeping on the ray between the Brazilian base-station and the target shells, perhaps using a sloughed membrane to provide the stable reversion line as a homing bird uses a shed feather. The male turtle may merely tag along in a protective role.

Georges Lakhovsky alluded to radio interference which disrupted the homing orientation of a flock of pigeons. They had been released close to a radio station's aerials during transmission on 2 July 1924 at Paterna, near Valencia in Spain. The birds were quite unable to find the home bearing,

and kept on flying in their direction-assessing circles. This
experiment was repeated several times with the same result.[8]
It seems possible that the frequency of the chemical
interchange control system coincided with a harmonic of
the radio station's frequency and was thus jammed, or that
the construction or alignment of the radio station's aerial
systems produced suppressive force-fields in our context.

When such untoward conditions as radio interference or
electric storms jam a chemical ray-path the flight must land
where it can and rest until normal conditions return. Then,
by fresh excretion, the migration direction on the shorter
route may be recovered and a second leg of the flight
commence. The forced, intermediate halt means that the
overall course is not necessarily the original great-circle direct
one but is now plotted at two stages, angled at the junction.

Apart from forced landings two or more stage migrations
accommodate birds which cannot sustain a very long journey
in a single flight. Veterans have provided valuable staging
posts, by shedding feathers at such junctions, and they lead
novices to these with unerring accuracy until the latter
become veterans by the same means.

Some sea-birds' food is not always available in a constant
quality all the year round. The necessity for obtaining
suitable nourishment during the local seasonal recession
governs fish population movements. The seasonal stimulation
of the distant environment which causes increased chemical
intensity in the metabolic changes in marine and riverine
creatures triggers the spawning impulse. Shoal movements are
then motivated by the incidence of fry and plankton. These
changes in radiational intensity are at once perceived by both
predatory fish and sea-birds, which are linked through the
same food chemicals shared by both. Hitherto it has been
thought that smell alone must, in some vague way, govern
the distant location of new food sources. Roy Bedichek, an
authority on the sense of smell, points out that odour
molecules are heavy and stay close to the ground.[9] This
appears to rule out smell as the guide to distant food sources
for winged creatures in general, and certainly where the
vast distances of migratory flight are concerned. Bedichek
continues: 'away down the smelling scale are birds, despite the

superstition among some hunters that ducks have a keen sense of smell.'[10] The ducks' keen sensorial ability to resonate with the chemical emissions of their hunters has, perhaps, led to this mis-attribution to smell.

Where fish are grouped, sometimes in territories, there are strong chemical rays linking them to other creatures sharing their characteristic food vibration rates (such as fish-hunting birds). When they leave the magnetic protection of suppressive seaweed forms to take part in chemically exposed shoals fish are acting out a strong compulsion. Observation suggests that the shoal is a co-operative device for finding concentrations of a food supply — such as minutiae congregating near rocks or weed, or masses of fry — solely by this chemical detection method. The tranquil, almost stationary, centre- and rear-ranks of grey-mullet shoals just offshore, form the base-terminus which becomes chemically linked with the littoral food sources under chemical scrutiny. The leaders of the shoal gyrate across the front ranks of the quiescent mullet mass, seeking the chemical links joining the mass to the prey which they can resonantly intercept.[11] Mackerel shoals often indulge in similar movements. During such co-operative chemical hunts for sprats, and so on, the shoal members will ignore any individual bait cast right in their path or into their midst by rock fishermen. When in this state, sight and smell seem to be temporarily overruled by chemical sensing.

Lepidoptera are superbly equipped with extraordinarily sensitive antennae. Rutherford Platt describes them as flexible in the wind and able to change their direction 'to pick up the mysterious messages that come from all directions through the air'.[12] He continues: 'the mosquito's antennae not only pick up incredibly tiny sounds but also select what it wants to hear'.[13] But the sensorial response to vibrations need not be to sound waves. Few, if any, lepidoptera live long enough to make a long return journey from a food migration flight by homing, for instance, on a personal item such as a discarded chrysalis. So these one-way migrants depend entirely on the familiar but now intensified chemical food vibrations issuing from fresh pasturages which are approaching their maximum signal in distant lands. The food chemicals in the insect's body resonate in sympathy when it crosses a line joining the waning pasturage and the new one far away.

Once an insect migration has started, the distant plantation's span, end- or side-on to the approaching flight, is linked with the lateral spread of the old base-plantation's limits. This determines the width of the insect fronts. The chemical compulsion to keep within the side-bounds of the two plantations' linked ray-paths accounts for the up-and-over reaction of winged insects to physical obstacles, as described by Dr C.B. Williams. [14]

A very interesting temporary departure from the direct ray-path lines is cited by Dr Williams, referring to the track of a narrow stream of Monarch butterflies migrating to the South in September 1935, as reported by a Mr Carr: 'The insects throughout the day turned suddenly to the E. at one point and then suddenly back to south at a second point about 200 yards away.' [15] It was mentioned that this change of course took place near the edges of a lake.

Two possible explanations can be offered for this diversion in chemical control terms. The most likely explanation is that at the diversion point the original north/south ray-paths crossed, or were overlapped by, another front system radiating from east to west linked to other geographical plantations containing the same fodder. This may have tempted the leaders to turn aside to assess the radiational quality of the newly encountered ray-paths. Having decided against a change of ray-path the flight then reverted to the original north/south orientation.

Some mirror-diversion experiments I set up indicate another, if less likely, possibility. In the case Carr reported the sun could have strongly illuminated the lake's sides. Some shining metal object may have caused reflections which might have 'relayed' the chemical signals and indicated a spurious direction. If this had tempted the diversion, then when the reflecting spot had been passed and the spurious direction signals were lost the flight would have reverted to the genuine north/south ray-paths. In both cases the reversion to the original north/south ray-paths would have to happen before the flight had wandered beyond the side limits of the ray-bands formed by both front and rear plantations.

For the mirror-diversion experiment a Large White cabbage butterfly was used. Some of its wing-powder was smeared on to a Brussels-sprout plant, and the insect's body, minus one wing which was retained as the matcher for the instrument's aerials, was placed on a table (Figure 1.2(a)). The direct personal ray-path connecting the body with the smeared plant was instrumentally identified and the ray-path followed towards the plant. Next, two mirrors were so arranged that the direct line from the insect's body to the powder-smeared plant was blocked or diverted and ceased to signal (Figure 1.2(b)). However, the reflected ray-paths AB and BC formed two new links between the butterfly and the powder-smeared plant, being relayed through a wide angle. Both new links when tested were found to be carrying the insect's unique signal.

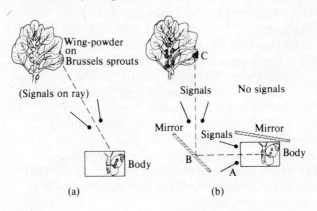

Figure 1.2 Mirror diversion of butterfly's ray-path

Those species of flora which depend solely upon pollination by lepidoptera may benefit from the personal factor in their chemical signals during the period immediately after the arrival of the insects at the target plantation. The pilot, or earliest-opening, flowers, by lowering their petal and sepal suppressive defences, have initiated and controlled the timing and fronts of the entire flight. In instances cited by Dr Williams,[16] the insects have been drawn by the released nectar and pollen radiations over some 1,900 miles in distance with heights of up to 3,000 feet to be surmounted. Each plant competes within its species for biological consummation. The individual seduction of an insect by flowers occurs at close quarters. Chemical quality affects vividness of colour and pungency of scent. Observation shows that an insect will not always alight on every flower it encounters. After hovering within the radiational epicentre around the flower, assessing its chemical quality, the insect then decides whether to succumb to the temptation or to move on.

Each insect leaves a minute smear of its body- or wing-powder on the plant, thus establishing a personal link with it. Also, in the course of that initial visit the insect receives pollen attachments containing the plant's unique imprint. This powder and pollen exchange is continued during the insect's physical contact with many flowers on its first circuits. The insect uses the place where it perches at night as the base-station from which it will be chemically guided in revisiting those plants it touched on the first day. Thus dual links of control are established from that place to each plant, and these are extended by each of the flowers visited, which now act as relay stations guiding the insect's repeat sequence. Repeat visits give the flowers pollination insurance.

Wild creatures which cannot migrate in order to replace a local seasonal deficiency in their particular diet must entrust their survival as a species to hibernation, to the use of 'queens', or to storage methods. Hibernators are awakened by the growing intensity of vibrational strength from food chemical emissions during early spring, a signal change which also stimulates the queens to start laying.

The stimulus which oscillates all chemicals through its impact on them (even deep below solid ground when it is not suppressed) seems to be secondary cosmic radiation deriving from the sun and stars. The intensity of this stimulus, and thus its effect on the matter being oscillated, varies according to season, time of day and year and geographical location. So the sun's apparent daily and yearly course plays a significant radiational and magnetic part in bringing about optimum conditions for the employment of these purposeful chemical links between flora and fauna. Also, of course, the sun gives creatures a general orientation both through its apparent visible position and thermal stimulus. But to suppose that wild creatures use the sun and stars as operational signposts for homing on to pin-point targets over thousands of kilometres is to indulge in anthropomorphic sophistry.

George de la Warr found that the emissions of persons and chemical deposits are linked with their photographs.[17] It is a characteristic of photographic emulsion, silver halides, that it traps nuclear emissions and can be used to trace and measure such bombardments. Commenting on this G. and A. Beiser state that 'it is the particle's electric charge which does the trick'.[18] I found, through many Revealer experiments, that the links between an organism and its blood, feather, hair, egg-shells, nails, bones (even after death), sputum, perspiration, excrement, and so on, could be instrumentally detected. It was also found that the photograph broadcasts the general chemical composition of the organism as well as its personal signal, both of which affected the Revealer's response when the appropriate matching samples were applied to the instrument's aerial systems. The organism is thus automatically linked with its dispersed photographs as well as with feather, hair or blood, all of which resonate with the owner's body. However, the separated bodily portions or photographs do not inter-link between themselves over distant ray-paths although they can be matched, one to another, when approached within the 1·25 metres epicentre around them. Similarly, it was found that the subject is linked with its voice, or even with heavy breathing, on a tape-recording. The unique signal of an individual, re-broadcast by his or her photograph, survives re-transmission over television when that screen is re-photographed. It was further found that a voice or tape-recording, when transmitted by telephone and re-recorded, maintains the link with the voice owner.

After successful experiments in detecting the signals re-broadcast from the subject matter in silver-halide emulsion photographs, I sought corroboration from Veale through his tests on photographs. These were sent to him concealed in wrappings so that he would be unaware of the likely metallic 'contents' of the items in the photographs. His results confirmed beyond all doubt the Revealer's capacity to 'read' the re-broadcasts from the photographs. I then began experiments attempting to locate distant people by means of their photographs and the Revealer. Such a system requires neutralization of the transmission of the operator's personal signals while retaining the power of his searching vector, over which the unique signals of the person sought can be then superimposed. Carbon pencil- or trade-marks on the back of a photographic print should be suppressed with a pencilled circle or ellipse, accurately drawn but not impressed into the print. This prevents the carbon trade-mark from resonating with other carbon and confusing the experiment.

The tests with the butterfly (Figure 1.2) had shown how a mirror could form a link with a creature's shed debris. In the same way a mirror, or a pack of shiny cooking-foil, could similarly initiate a ray-path leading directly to a person's body when the reflector was set at an accommodating angle and faced its direction. This would replace the hair (or other) base-station, and could also pick up the signals of any other organism that it faced. Also it had the advantage of easy and controlled altitude adjustment in order to pick up the subject's radiation when reflected from the ionospheric layers. It could also be mounted at the centre of a compass-rose or bearing-board marked in degrees.

In order to develop a basic method for locating missing persons through their emitted personal signals, the placing of similarly uniquely signalling organic specimens at points of known distance and elevation was the next step. The object was to obtain practice and to find out if a range-finding principle were possible. It was arranged that the specimens should be placed on certain lighthouses when they were paid service visits. The specimens eventually stretched from the Eddystone to Pendeen lighthouses, including those within these distance limits and those within the Isles of Scilly group. The heights at which each specimen had been placed above mean sea-level were recorded. The specimens used were half mussel-shells of which the other halves, carefully labelled, were retained as the matchers.

Captain Harry Harvey, a retired sea captain who taught at the Newlyn School of Navigation, helped with the earliest experiments and some great-circle calculations for various ports around the world. The observatory was Captain Harvey's back garden 280 feet above Sennen Cove. He adapted his sextant to act as an 'artificial terminus' or base-station by removing the front mirror while retaining the rear one attached to the movable arm over the calibrated arc. The sextant was then attached to a mast. I then found the ray-path, indicating the general direction, of each lighthouse specimen when I passed in front of the sextant, which was periodically moved around to face various directions. Then by adjusting the mirror angle, one could momentarily lose and momentarily regain the signals, noting the readings of both adjustments. The figures thus obtained with the one sextant mirror had to be halved to arrive at readings in degrees, minutes and seconds. However, as it turned out, the differences in heights above sea-level of the specimens in the lighthouses precluded any accurate comparisons over these short distances. It became clear that no range-finding progression towards a target could be achieved by this method beyond the distance of the curvature of the earth. Nevertheless these experiments did pave the way for a method of limiting range and thus eliminating signals from land masses beyond and in front of a now isolated area.

The next step was to explore methods of identifying the centre line of the invisible ray joining the artificial terminus reflector to the lost person, so that a more accurate bearing could be deduced. This had to be guessed when the Revealer antennae rods appeared to be set at a perfect V-displacement. I made a 'Farfinder' and a ray-centring aid, and a sketch-plan for a revolving frame to carry them around a central pillar. Veale made the frame from plumber's plastic tubing and mounted it on Shepherd castors. The object of this experiment was to locate the direction of the Trinity House vessel *Stella* by means of a photograph of the master, Captain Tarrant. Veale and I were invited to demonstrate the method to Lt-Commander Douglas RN, Deputy Chief Coastguard. First, Veale showed how a piece of that officer's hair matched with his uniform cap which was placed on the floor and approached within the 1·25 metres distance. Also he showed how the unexposed film in a camera did not resonate with the officer until his photograph had been taken and

24

undeveloped film was broadcasting his personal signal. One coastguard, who had previously got wind of the experiments at Tol-pedn, came forward with a sizeable hank of hair that he had shorn from his wife's head: one hair would have sufficed. He wanted to know where she was. Veale went around the artificial terminus with the hair on the Revealer aerials and, having found the general direction, pointed into the distance. 'Over there,' he said. 'Good,' said the coastguard. 'That means that she's home at St Just.'

It was now time to try and find the direction of *Stella* via the master's photograph. When Veale and I had both tried this, and had decided on our best ray-centre approximations, verification had to be sought. Captain Tarrant was asked to plot his own position and pass on the result. His position, reconciled with the charts, showed that my own reading was about 6° out of reckoning but that Veale's was only 4° out. Considering the errors inherent in the gear perhaps these pioneer results were not too bad. An article on the experiment was published in the Board of Trade magazine, *Coastguard*,[19] but the matter was not pursued further.

Lawrence Veale died in July 1968, and the onset of a terminal illness in my own family just afterwards precluded any further experimental work with the Revealer until the middle of 1970. The placing of about eighty half mussel-shell markers in ports all over the world was the preliminary step for the continuation of this locating principle, now named the 'V-ray' method as a compliment to Veale. Ports were chosen for these signalling specimens because only the height of a ship's deck at high and low water would be the altitude variable in this respect. In some instances the mussel-shell markers were placed to form links in chains, a system of radiational stepping-stones for a range-limiting experiment.

The reflector of the Farfinder ancillary apparatus is tilted back so as to receive the signals from the station farthest away in a chain — say Port Stanley, Falkland Islands. By gradually reducing the tilt of the reflector's angle, and testing with that mussel-shell matcher, Port Stanley's signal is marginally lost. The range now scrutinized for a ship's signals is less than Port Stanley's distance from the observatory. The next station in a chain, away from Port Stanley, Rio Grande do Sul, is then lost by the same method of depressing the reflector's angle, and so on. Another method of reducing the range, this time from the observatory's end, enabled the chain stations to be progressively lost in the outwards direction also: that is, when Portsmouth's or Beachy Head's mussel signals are lost, then the search area must be clear of the British south coast and over the sea. Some limit-station chains established with mussel-shell markers are as follows:

Chain 1   Portsmouth; St Peter Port; Corunna; Fayal; Funchal; Las Palmas; St Vincent, CVI; Recife; Santos; Rio Grande do Sul; Port Stanley, FI

Chain 2   Pevensey Castle; Cagliari; Marsa Xlocx, Malta; Ras Azir; Goa; Colombo; Cocos (Keeling) Is; Singapore; Perth, WA; Melbourne; Brisbane; Suva.

Chain 3   Pevensey Castle; Cagliari; Bizerta; Mogadishu (Ras Azir distance arc); Mombasa; Mahé, Seychelles; Mozambique (Tamatave arc); Durban.

Chain 4   Valentia, S. Eire; Fayal; St Johns, Newfoundland; Halifax, NS; Bermuda; Norfolk, Virginia; Georgetown, Guyana; Colon, Panama.

The theory for working this limit-station method is this. Let us suppose that a ship, to be identified and located either through its captain's photograph or a placed organic marker, is sailing between the distance arcs of Fayal and Funchal (chain 1). After picking up the ship's direction, using the retained matcher, the outwards limit control is set to just lose the Portsmouth arc and the continuance of the ship's signal verified. This procedure continues, station by station, until Fayal's signal is just lost and the ship's is still received. If, then, Funchal's signal and the ship's are both lost the device is retracted to regain Fayal's signal. Reduction of the limit stations is then started in the homewards direction by progressively declining the artificial terminus reflector, checking for the ship after each station's signal loss. When the Funchal signal is just lost (in the homewards direction) and the ship continues to signal, then the ship is between the

distance arcs of Fayal and Funchal. In another instance by
losing the signals from markers placed down the East African
coast in the outwards direction, and losing those from
Singapore to Perth in the homewards direction, a chemical
ray search could be restricted to the Indian Ocean. This
would enable monitoring of shipping.

While I can foresee some good uses of the limit-station
method it is not the system which would be best for locating
persons missing at sea. For that purpose triangulation from
chosen coastguard stations at each end of the longest datum
lines that the British Isles can afford would be the most
suitable method. Photographs of lost persons, or even their
voices on tape taken from Mayday calls, would be televised
over closed circuits to be developed at the participating
coastguard stations or transmitted to them by telephone to
be re-taped. The resulting direction bearings would be
computed at a centre and a search area indicated to the air-sea
rescue teams. This could reduce the enormous waste in time
and expense of random searches.

Some further discoveries have helped towards an eventual
working system for locating missing persons and for
monitoring ships' courses since those early days at Tol-Pedn.
A method of pin-pointing over a mineral deposit or over a
ray-path's centre can now be used so that the former, chancy
visual estimates of a centre line can be discarded. A filter has
been found which appears to eliminate the multiplication of
spurious direction signals through mirrors or shining car-
bumpers between or behind the sought person and the
apparatus. These experiments indicate that the unwanted
mirror gremlin can be overcome with this filter while the
genuine signal, direct from the organism's body, will still
come through the filter unimpaired.

4 Sir Kenelm Digby and his sympathetic powder

In August 1973, some hydrangea cuttings were taken from
two separate shrubs in a neighbour's garden. These, when
potted and tested, disclosed their links with their individual
parent plants. About a week after labelling and potting, tests

showed the persistence of those parental-scion links. In September, when fresh shoots had just appeared, further tests showed that they had achieved radiational individuality, as the former links with the parent shrubs had disappeared. Some sycamore seeds were then subjected to similar tests.

Sycamore seeds planted on 25 September 1973 remained linked with the parent tree for at least twenty days. When re-tested on 17 October the radiational separation of tree and seeds, over the personal link, had been completed. Other tests had shown that, as with fauna, the personal links between a plant, its leaf, seed or scion, are maintained not only over the shorter route but also in global circumambience the opposite way around the world. The time-lag in the latter instance is also about 30 seconds — similar to the tests on faunal subjects. It has been noticed that these times vary slightly, presumably owing to the periodic rise and fall of the deflecting ionospheric levels, which variations affect the distances covered by the particle flow.

The general purpose of these links seems to be parental support of the weaker resources of separated seed or scion by means of an energizing entropic bombardment, when chemical sustenance or stimuli are directed over the personal link, perhaps in order to maintain healthy cellular oscillation before the roots appear and are able to extract chemical nutriment from the soil. It may be, in effect, a radiational umbilical-cord system. A test on one pair of human identical twins showed that they were not radiationally identical as their personal signals did not match each other's. Opportunity has not yet offered for tests on more pairs of such twins. As they are separate developments from the same fertilized but split ovum, this radiational distinction must surely be due to a minute difference in the chemical balance of nutriment conveyed to each embryo, via the umbilical cords of the mother, at a crucial stage in their vertebral formation. A test on Siamese twins should be very interesting. If each identical twin's radiationally different personal signal is fixed by a minute imbalance in chemical absorption, then a seedling's radiational uniqueness, among a batch of others rooted from the same fertilized seed-pod, can only be due to minute differences in the chemical composition of each soil spot. If this is so, then radiational uniqueness in both flora and fauna is due solely to environmental chemical causes. This also seems to imply that the determination of a chick's, a caterpillar's or a spawn unit's radiational individuality also depends on the different balance of chemicals in each egg from the same clutch or batch.

Wild animals keep themselves chemically supplied through the exercise of this sense. The domesticated dog which licks its owner's hand is obtaining the chemicals, exuded from the human skin, which they both contain. (This does not, of course, imply that the dog and owner derive no other satisfactions from this act.) Also, as noted above, a dog will bite selected grasses when it perceives that it is getting low on a specific item on account of its domesticated life. The chewed grass plant homes into the dog's mouth by means of the deposited saliva until leached away by rain.

When testing other people for biochemical tissue-salt sufficiency or deficiency with the Revealer it is essential that the operator maintains his own full complement of these checked items. Through frequent experiments on myself, relatives and friends, I found that, when a deficiency in a specific item was detected, it was not necessary for the subject to swallow corrective tablets. The saliva, dribbled on to the corrective tablets and placed in a sterile test-tube, homes into the saliva glands or cells of the mouth from which it came. In the homing process the necessary corrective 'dose' of the compound in the tube is conducted into that person's body, 'riding' on the saliva's homing waves. So the soluble corrective tablets are placed in the test-tube, copiously salivated upon and then securely corked with a new cork: two of the tablets in the tube are sufficient. The test-tube should be placed in a horizontal position and not accidentally suppressed by any intervening sign-form between it and the owner's body. When the person has absorbed enough of the corrective radiations from this bombardment the body automatically rejects further absorption. By the third or fourth day, when another check is made with the Revealer, it is usually found that the body's radiations are restored on the items formerly deficient. After a period of about two months the test-tube may show signs of fermentation. Though this is self-generated and harmless, the test-tube should be washed out and sterilized against future use. It seems that the higher potential of energy radiated by the concentrated chemical tablets, soaked in the subject's saliva, directs that energy flow towards the weaker, starved tissues in the subject's throat. It has been postulated that it is entropy which directs a one-way flow of energy from a stronger to a weaker deposit. On no account should allopathic drugs be conducted into the body in this way as there is no means to control the dose.

An account of Sir Kenelm Digby's 'Sympathetic powder' cure in the seventeenth century came to hand after these experiments were made.[20] His curative salves were applied to the bloodstains on the bandage from a wound and not directly to the wound itself. The results were reported as rapid and soothing, and aroused the keen interest of King James and the Royal Physician.

It was decided to try Digby's method using modern antiseptics and several treatments have been tried for cuts on fingers, ankles and toes. On each occasion the very rapid healing of even a very deep cut was completely free from any suppuration which so often accompanies the healing of a cut treated by direct medicaments. Immediately after a cut the free flow of blood from the damaged cells inside the wound was staunched with a bandage. Within a few minutes the bandage was taken off and placed in a solution of TCP and water (TCP happened to be the antiseptic to hand). The bandage was then laid on top of a reversed saucer (it should not be placed within a sign-suppressive round bowl). A plaster is then placed over the wound, which has not been touched with any antiseptic, merely to keep out grit. On one occasion where a bad chisel cut had been suffered the thus treated patient reported an initial sharp stinging of the wound just after the removed bandage had been treated. In this case an amount of neat TCP had been applied to the blood on the bandage. The next day this bad cut had lightly healed over, with no suppuration. In another case, when a boy had skinned his big toe on the beach, a pad of dry cotton wool was gently pressed on to the skinned area to gather some personal, exuded matter. A half-and-half solution of TCP and water was applied to the cotton wool after the boy had gone to his room. At the moment the antiseptic was applied to the cotton wool the boy called out that his toe was stinging. Pending any acceptable scientific explanation, may one suggest that the Digby treatment is effective because the homing conductance penetrates the skin and reaches the inner, damaged tissues or cells whence the blood first came, whereas a surface treatment with medicaments would not reach those inner tissues owing to both the skin's elasticity and its congealed surface?

Post-operational infection frequently occurs despite sterile operating-theatre conditions and wound-dressings. New medical evidence assigns the cause of this to 'internally' released microbic infection, but this may also be a result of the homing conductance phenomenon. The section surgically removed from the patient's body automatically continues to home in on the contiguous, damaged cells in the body area from which it came. Should the removed section come into contact with infected matter, at any time prior to its radiational neutralization or to the advanced healing process, it seems that the infection could be conducted into the patient's surgically wounded cells via the homing ray-link. A preventive drill would be very simple to carry out. The removed section and all stained dressings would be totally immersed, immediately, in an unsuppressed container holding a diluted solution of, say, TCP. These items, in their antiseptically soaked state, would then be sealed in a plastic bag to await final destruction. The stinging effect in the wound, proportional to the solution strength of the ray-conducted TCP, would soon pass. An additional line of defence against such radiationally conducted infection would be to protect the patient in his bed for a few days by means of a quincunx radiational pyramid.

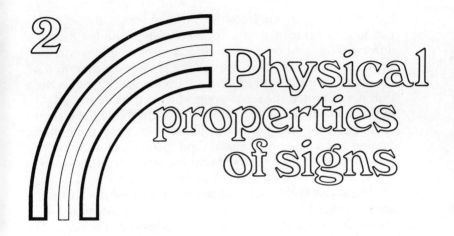

2 Physical properties of signs

1 Palaeolithic cave art

Thousands of years before the advent of religion, sanctuary
was recognized by early man as being a physical reality,
not as the psychic abstraction it was to become in mediaeval
Europe. Reflexive response to sympathetic particle- or wave-
interchange in the chemical radiating regions of the spectrum
was the birthright of early man before he allowed that sense
to degenerate. Chemical interchange may be defined as the
resonant interplay between identical chemical deposits
separated by distance. Just as the chemicals which a wild
creature contains in its body must be renewed from the
natural supply in its environment, so early man also found
his distant food's direction through his sensory response to
the rays linking him to such chemical sources. Modern man
is the Ishmael of the animal kingdom. He, alone among
sentient creation, cannot respond to chemical exchange,
which provides the main communication system for all flora
and fauna. With the possible exceptions of the Australian
aboriginal and the Bushman, or that timeless link with
natural man, the water-diviner, he is unaware of this latent,
physical sense. The spontaneous chemical projections and the
received responses which primitive man enjoyed when
hunting for animals and plants may have deteriorated through

33

lack of practice in late Neolithic times. A long consolidating period of tribal settlements, local cultivation and the partial domestication of herds, entailing grain storage and winter curing of meat, may have assisted the gradual degeneration of the chemical interchange faculty. Farming developments may thus have blunted the sense upon which a tribe depended in the nomadic life, a state of existence enforcing the distant sensing and following of herds. Those herds were, themselves, sensing and moving to seasonal food maturing in different areas in turn. It may be urged that the loss of a sense would take hundreds of thousands of years, as with bodily modifications such as the tail or shrunken appendix. If that were so, then the gradual deterioration of the chemical-perception sense might be the cause rather than the result of Neolithic farming.

Seasonal migrations are chemically inspired from great distances. The spring increase of metabolic activity in food plants and in related migrating fauna occurs in widely separated geographical areas in turn. The rising intensity of signal strength in each locality awakens the hibernators and stimulates insect queens to lay. The radiational couriers carry bulletins concerning the chemical readiness of distant pasturage, the issue of invitations to pollinate and other up-to-date news concerning variations of intensity, all of which are vital to the successful foraging of flora's faunal dependants. Homing and the distant location of prey depend also on accurate chemical direction. However, if there were no counter to faunal searching vectors projected by every hunting creature, most species would have become extinct long ago, having been systematically exterminated by a succession of unrestricted predators drawn from great distances to the young shoots of a plantation or to the eggs of bird colonies.

Nature's conservation counter to the hunting vector lay in the evolution of certain two-dimensional signs and three-dimensional sign-structures, of which flora may have first produced the archetypes in the twig and leaf. The natural suppressors of food signals throw a protective mantle of paramagnetic force-fields over or around each plant or resting animal, suppressing the involuntary broadcast of untimely pollination advertisement or self-betraying protein radiation.

Arboreal man employed the protective effects of fortuitously found crossed twigs and leaf-pattern alignments to confine his chemical emissions which would otherwise have betrayed his presence; primitive man was constantly exposed to distant detection by ferocious animals, especially during unguarded times of rest. Palaeolithic and Mesolithic man — by observation, experiment and practice — discovered artificial applications of the natural archetypes of crossed twigs, leaves, fishbones and feathers, by testing their suppressive effects. By painting or engraving the basic form of a protective sign on their walls they worked to achieve a chemical anonymity or 'invisibility'. This chemical invisibility on a predator's monitoring system was to pass into myth as optical invisibility with which story-tellers in later ages fascinated their audiences.

Tests with crosses, circles and pits cut in firm, unmarked beach sand were made in Cornwall in 1970. These showed how paramagnetic suppression can be initiated and employed. Models made of wood and Plasticine, incorporating the basic features of temples and shrines, showed the effectiveness of certain sign-forms in completely blocking the passage of the chemical radiation to which the Revealer operator responds. As it is simply the structure of a sign which is operative in this context it may be made of any homogeneous material such as bone, wood, stone, metal, textile, pottery, or modern industrial plastics such as celluloid.

A suppressive sign or sign-structure must be placed above, below, around or between an emitting source and its exact chemical correspondent. The magnetic screen formed by a sign lies along a very thin plane and is effective according to its physical alignment with the otherwise interchanging mineral deposits, or between creatures carrying similar chemicals. Up to certain limits the suppressive force-field around a sign increases with its visible size. However, the ratio of force-field extension is diminished with a sign's progressive enlargement. For example, the long axis of the capital X on my typewriter was measured at 2·5 mm; its suppressive force-field radius is approximately 11·5 cm. An average leaf of the bay-tree, *Lauris nobilis*, measuring 9 cm, showed a suppressive force-field radius of 34·5 cm. Slight variations which occur at different times of the day and season are apparently due to changes in cosmic-radiation intensity. Such suppressive signs prevent horizontal correspondence between like-chemicals when they are interposed in the vertical position. When horizontally deployed they block the usual correspondence of like-chemicals in the vertical plane.

The void or pit-edge signals encountered when approaching a natural fissure or a man-made pit or grave cause an outwards swing of the Revealer's rods; that is, they move away from the centre of the operator's body. This effect is the opposite to that produced when the rods are over a signalling mineral or metal; then they cross inwards. An apparent magnetic repulsion, which may be contributory to the outwards-turning posture when over the edge of a pit, may be due to a positive charge encountered at that cut in the subsoil. It may be that the magnetic hiatus left in the subsoil at the moment of the cut needs the insertion of a positive charge to re-link the momentarily separated sections of the weak, negative-charged continuum of the earth's magnetic field. This speculation appears to account for what happens when experiments are made with suppressors made of bamboo sticks placed over pits. No suppression is achieved by one, two, or three sticks laid in the same direction over the pit or its edges. To suppress the signals issuing from the edges the magnetic screen must be a self-contained unit made up of either four, or a multiple of four, sticks of the same chemical composition lying approximately in the same direction, or of any number of sticks which are overlaid by at least one other to form a cross or lattice.

The motifs encountered in Palaeolithic cave art provide the strongest evidence that man consciously adapted nature's twig-signs to control the chemical interchange phenomenon. Using the stick lattice he deliberately suppressed the emissions from the edges of pits to prevent approaching animals from otherwise sensing them. The signs essential to produce suppressive pit-covers were functionally illustrated in paintings or engravings on his cave walls as hunting

instructions. However, they may also have had the incidental
effect of screening those areas of the walls from a predator's
searching vector, much as modern man uses curtains to
screen himself from light or sound waves.

Magdalenian man's trapping and cave-insulation techniques
were based on his technological achievement of an artificial
lattice suppressor, as is shown in the caves at Lascaux
(Figure 2.1). The hunting method was to prepare pits in
places where the configuration of the terrain would compel
the animals to take a narrow path, preferably bounded on
the far side by a cliff face or other flanking obstacle. For
descriptive clarity the delineation of the pit-cover had to
show its essential suppressive construction. When in place
it would be concealed from vision with grasses and leaves.

Figure 2.1 Lascaux caves: technical murals

The artist shows darts being shot in showers, perhaps not so
much in hope of killing the animal as goading it in the
desired direction. The artist is also at pains to illustrate that
the animals would place their hooves with confidence over
the non-radiating pit edges. The operational detail of the
Lascaux murals suggests that the use of suppressive pit-fall
covers may have been novel. Their depiction also protected
certain areas of the cave walls, and may have provided a
sanctuary from the dangers of the outside predatory world.

The Dome of Serpents at Rouffignac[1] which was heavily
engraved with serpent-forms in Aurignacian times some
thousands of years prior to the Lascaux murals, may have
pioneered the latter art and science of insulating the
sanctuary. It seems likely that the discovery of the physically
protective force-field cast by the serpentine sign was made
by casual tracing of patterns with a stick on the surface of

soft ground, or sand, beneath which lay a radiating mineral deposit. The emissions from below ground would then cease to reach the chemically sensitive artist when the site was thus overlaid with the serpentine sign. It may be that such drawing was inspired by observing the snake's movement or its tracks left in sand. Inevitably, human recognition of the protective characteristic of the sign's own value would be transferred to the living snake. Long after the loss of man's chemical reflex faculty, the serpentine sign's dimly remembered protective use may have been mythologized into a spiritual emanation from the creature, and played its part in serpent cults.

At Aldeaquemada, Jaen, in Spain, we find further evidence of the use of magnetic protection techniques.[2] The stylized figures described as humanoid, which are painted in those caves, seem to be further experiments in breaking the automatic chemical links between man and his predatory enemies outside the cave. In the humanoid figures the circles, suggesting bodies, are traversed by vertical lines. These form crosses at two points at the circumference of each circle which vastly extends the magnetic coverage, as a cross throws a radius of suppression well beyond its visible limits while a circle only protects the area within its circumference. If the humanoid epithet is a valid description of these paintings then the message appears to be: 'This is how we can prevent our presence in here being sensed from outside.' These humanoid figures also appear to be harbingers of future sanctuary guardians who, wearing pectoral crosses or discs, were to be the keepers of a technique based on the applied science of their race and time. Here may be the origin of ritual, based firmly on a technical reality, which was to survive long after the physical effectiveness of the protective use of signs had faded from the conscious minds of men. We may come to the conclusion that cave-painting and cave-engraving were functional, in as much as the accurate depiction of sign-structure was the prime consideration. We have noted the serpentine-form suppressors on the Dome at Rouffignac. One writer, doubting the assignment of some roof-engraving at Lascaux to aesthetic consciousness, nevertheless remarks: 'it is difficult to explain . . . the numerous engravings on the small dome overlooking the mouth of the Shaft of the Dead Man.'[3] Indeed it seems likely that aesthetic consciousness did play a minor role in instructional cave art when the essential sign detail, which ensured the physical containment of man's own betraying chemical emissions within the cave ceiling, as well as within its walls, was one criterion of achievement. Inner-dome protective embellishment was to find its apotheosis in the edifice of Santa Sophia.

The effective alignments of a cross suppressor are similarly deployed in nature. Plant leaves are aligned according to the need either to project or allow the uninhibited chemical radiation, or to inhibit it. Their signals follow the direction of arteries and veins and issue from a leaf's edges. Its broad surface, when placed at right angles to chemical ray-paths, interrupts interchange.

There are two kinds of suppressors employed in nature: those which afford local suppression, limited to the visible boundaries of, say, an egg-shell; and those whose force-fields extend far beyond the visible limits of a sign such as the cross. A classified selection of familiar signs, developed by man for religious purposes, is shown in Figure 2.3.

The Gravettian period of the Palaeolithic Age had produced portable objects carrying more elaborate signs such as the 'open cross' and chevrons. These are shown on some 'Venus' prototype idols (Figure 2.2). The protective virtue physically inherent in the sign itself was to be attributed, in later times, to the object which bore that sign.

Wide-extent suppressive artefacts could be arranged in the fissures of cave walls or ceilings so that their force-fields would overlap to cover, say, the sleeping area. Such portable suppressors could be used in the casual shelters occupied by nomads during their seasonal wanderings. Regular migration posting-stations, or settlements, would be permanently sign-protected sanctuaries. The effigies of gods- and saints-in-the-niche are the lineal descendants of this category of signed idols and are also themselves magnetically protected within the architectural niche.

When protective signs were applied to animal-like or humanoid figures it indicated a growing belief in the protection bestowed by the very idols or graven images

Figure 2.2   Gravettian 'Venus'

which represented unseen powers which the signs identified.
Thus the sign, the name and its sound were merged into a
recognizable entity. Three distinct types of god-sign-sound
emerged. First, those which signalled, inviting the sympathy
and beneficence of a fertility god (Figure 2.3, column 1);
second, those which gave local suppression within the sign's
visible boundaries (column 2); and third, those which
provided wide-extent protection against the dangers of the
profane world and also shielded man against the unpredictable
malice of a higher, capricious god who was responsible for
nature's cataclysms (column 3). It will be noticed that the
signs of the serpent and the bull horns, both of which are
most efficient wide-extent suppressors, are properly assigned
to column 3 and not to the fertility or signalling column
(column 1).

The development of clay artefacts, embellished with
signs, indicates the threshold of man's rationalizing process
which, through the deterioration of his chemical reflex-
sense, led him to undervalue the natural radiation which
still produced some reaction from his nervous system. He
now began to reduce the functional magnetic-protective signs
derived from nature to perfunctory magico-religious protective
symbols. Portable idols, as well as fixed, sculpted ones, were
now firmly established as the deputies of shadowy
theriomorphic, therio-anthropomorphic, and

anthropomorphic gods in turn. Man's ancient and well-founded fear of predatory beasts was progressively rationalized by way of Egyptian religion to a fear of the rulers of Mount Olympus.

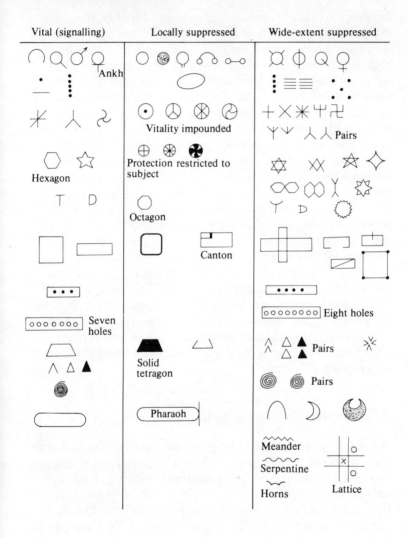

Figure 2.3   A selection of familiar signs, classified according to force-field character

From the Bronze Age onwards, the great mammalian and reptilian predators had long been discouraged and excluded by walls. So the terror of those predators which over millenia had permeated man's conscious collective mind was transferred at a subconscious level to a belief in demons, dragons and other capricious supernatural beings, notably the chthonic gods. It was these inimical forces against which sanctuary construction was now employed. Primitive man had understood only too clearly what the inimical forces were; perhaps he had been able even to perceive the probing vectors of the sabre-toothed tiger and other menacing beasts as small river fish sense the approach of a predatory pike. When in his sign-protected sanctuary he no longer vibrated under the impact of such searches for his chemical body-nourishment, and when he could no longer obtain any response to his own projected chemical vector, then he knew that the cave was safely insulated. Aeons of proto- and primitive man's arboreal and cave associations caused the residual memory of applied Palaeolithic and Mesolithic twig- and leaf-protection to sink to the subconscious level of, perhaps, Neolithic mental processes. These were partly exhumed and clothed in sacred tree myth and, much later, adorned religious protective structures. The seers, who still retained a degree of sensitivity after the general loss, became the adepts of the ancient arts and sciences. A priesthood of diviners followed, raising the ghost of the practical rites which were the core around which religious liturgy was to be wrapped.

2 The protective origin of script

An anthropomorphic god's sign-sound-name was regarded as the equivalent of the very god him- or herself, and that name was often protected by being confined within a circle, such as with the Egyptian god Re or Ra: $\odot$. Protection, here, may have been euphemism used to excuse man's impertinent attempts to impound a divine power against his departure to another tribe. On seasonal occasions, when the priest made contact with the god to request meteorological forecasts and dispensations for farming purposes, the ritual required a vital, unsuppressed altar. In such situations the priest used vital, signalling signs for rain and fertility stimulation and to encourage the yearly resurrection of the corn-god or goddess. A vital sign, the Ankh, was used by the Egyptians to secure the restoration of the living spirit. The six-limbed signalling star came to represent the holy energizing spirit. Vital signs which had assisted physical communion with the god now acquired psychic connotations.

The strong resemblance between the Azilian painted pebbles, South Spanish rock art and items in ancient scripts, aroused the interest of the French scholar, Piette. He pointed out the similarity to some ancient Mediterranean scripts, notably Phoenician and Greek[4]. A heavy numerical preponderance of suppressive signs over vital ones occurs in all ancient scripts and perhaps reflects man's continuous obsession with the sanctuary aspect of sign-protection. The functional ancestry of protective script can scarcely be denied when the Revealer shows that tested carbon signs perform in the same way as the tested structures encountered in leaf, feather and fish vertebrae. This explains why tree, bird and fish became eternal and ubiquitous religious symbols. The magnetic protection afforded by its signs became a benison offered by the plant or creature. The conceptual composites of angel, cherubim, seraphim, winged sphinx and sacred grove also owe their protective origins to the efficacy of their natural archetypes. Extensive Revealer tests with script signs drawn in graphite suggest coincidence as an unlikely reason for this phenomenon. The protective signs attached to syllables and prefixes in god, king, priest, holy place-names, liturgy and ritual, including furniture and clothing, occur regularly and ubiquitously in many different scripts and laguages. The sample of holy names considered below is mainly concerned with signs and sounds derived from the Indo-European sun-god roots Chi and Ti. Scripts other than those of that group have their own roots which also conform with the same principle of protection and which also extend to all religious practice and to holy localities. Some prehistoric signs and suppressive equivalents drawn from nature's archetypes and their associated Chi

Physical properties of signs

Mezin

Lascaux

Aldeaquemada

S. Spanish rock art

Azilian pebbles

Ku Wen Prehistoric*
to 800 BC   Chun   Shou   Mu   Chiang   Chung
             sovereign hand   tree   boundary   middle
Pa Fen Shu c. AD 100

Sumerian   * Sky god   Thunder mountain   + Protect

	CH	KS	KA	KH	H	J	GHA	E	S	SH	Z	D	T	TH	M	N	PH	PS	R	Q
Iberian													×		⊕					
Egyptian† hieroglyphs																				⊙
Ugaritic																				
Phoenician														⊕						Φ
Linear B			⊕																	
Corinth			×										⊕	M						
Modern Greek			×						Σ				⊙	M						
Coptic‡			χ																	
Arabic																				
Berber									3			+								
Mende				χ	⊕															
Brahmi			+		ε	ω							⊙							
Late Ku Wen																				
Wang Chao		×												+						
Kata Kana			カ					ω												
Siberian										Ψ	× 33									

Figure 2.4   Prehistoric signs of unknown phonemes and phonoglyphs
of similar suppressive signs

44

and Ti phonemes are compared in Figure 2.4.

In his Manx dictionary, compiled from the living Goidelic Celtic language that was still spoken during his childhood, the Reverend Juan Kelly lists An as a ring, Chen-An as the orb of fire of the sun and Chenney or Tienney as pure, elemental fire.[5] God was believed to dwell in the fire; that is, in the disc of the sun. Chiarn or Tiarn was a lord or prince; Chiamble or Teamble church or temple. Chi and Ti phonemes, tied to their suppressive script signs, are found everywhere in the religious context. They appear as prefixes or syllables in the names of holy places, kings and priests, specific religions, architectural features, ritual furniture and vestments, all bearing witness to their essential employment of magnetic protection through the signs' force-fields. There are, of course, variants of the ubiquitous Chi and Ti roots within the Indo-European group. Variations in guttural phonemes — such as C — arise from differences in local speech production and through diachronic modifications within each language in the group occurring over the course of time. The very young child, when learning to speak, usually avoids the difficult hard C or K sound in favour of the easier T. Referring to Grimm's 'law of sound shift' which 'illustrated the conversion of guttural Indo-European to Teutonic roots gh-g-k-h', Alfred Kallir included C,G,K,Q, partly also J,Y,F and Z, in this conversion system.[6] The world-wide distribution of holy names thus associated with guttural C and its modifications, and the Chi and Ti roots, offers strong support for the theory of race-dispersal from a common origin.

The Chen and Tien derivatives range from China to Chile. Choukoutien and Tientsin, Carchemish, Tarchuna, Chichester, Cheddar, Tintern, Tinwall (Baal's Fire) Chichen Itza, Cholula, Chincha Alta and Chicago are examples. Chi appears in North American Indian tribal names such as Chippewa, Cherokee, Choctaw, Chickawaw, Comanche, Apache; among others in modified form. The Cornish words for house, Chy and Ty, are considered, nowadays, as secular names. Place-names, so prefixed, should remind us of their original religious foundations which gave their names to the locality whatever secular use they were put to in later ages. Racial differences in speech production, among evolving races within the Indo-European group, produced many phonemes with both hard and soft variants of Chi and Ti roots.

The phoneme, Ch, is sounded as in church, chapel, chalice, chantry, charnel, etc.; it becomes hard Ki or Ka in Kynance, Kyoto, Cohen, Cantor, Canterbury, cathedral, cardinal, Ciudad, Kano, Kandy, Khartoum, Quito or Koran. Again, the hardening of Ch is extended to some tribal names such as Carib and Cree. A modified branch of the Ch-Ka development leads to Ga as in Ganges, Ganesha, Ghana, Guru, etc. On the other hand Ch can become soft Sh as in Chartres, Chamblandes, Shanghai, Shanklin, Shoshone, Shian or Cheyenne, and Shawnee. Sh, in its turn, is racially modified again in Semitic speech to Se or Z. The Bible offers the example of those Ephraimites, whose inability to aspirate the first 'h' in the test-word Shibboleth gave away their race and led to their slaughter at the hands of Jephthah's guards.[7] The Ti root also provides its list of racially modified derivatives; for example, the Greek Theo and Siamese Thai: Teotihuacan, Tyre, Tenkas, Timbuctoo and the Pope's Tiara.

A few god names and king-priest titles consolidate this allocation of magnetic-protective sound-signs: King, Kaiser, Tsar, Caesar, Cham, Cadi, Ching, Khan, Koning, Khedive, Caliph, Shah, Sheikh, Sherif, Shogun. Among the gods are Christ, Krishna, Vishnu, Shamash, Shiva, Kama, the Shinto gods, Kore, Kybele, Ishtar, Zeus, Tinia, Tanith.

In cuneiform script renderings of a king's name or a holy place-name the same magnetic protection operates. The inclusion of at least one wide-extent suppressive element is sufficient to cover the whole name, no matter how many vital signals are also present (Figure 2.5).

The technical challenge confronting the scribes of hieroglyphs, in their construction of protective signs for the divine and regal names, was the same in kind as for cuneiform and other scripts. It differed in degree only where the personal name of the Pharaoh was specifically delineated. As with all ancient scripts, royal and religious names contain suppressive characters which afford protection extending over the whole name, and beyond it. The locally suppressive cartouche, which uniquely shields the Pharaoh's personal name, and sometimes his godly attribution also, limits the range of the wide-extent suppressive signs which are already efficiently guarding that name. Its particular purpose, apart from establishing the king's visual isolation, was to localize his magnetic aura which, without the cartouche, would spread beyond his name: 'There's such divinity doth hedge a king' (Figure 2.6). This peculiar Egyptian device ensured, in a subtle manner, the withdrawal of the Pharaoh from any presumption by ordinary mortals whose names, also inscribed in the hieroglyphic epic, would otherwise bask in his widely spread protective aura. Gods' names were permitted to enter the cartouche to associate with the exclusive Pharaoh but it was a one-way movement. Pharaoh did not leave this royal-box shield. Other signs associated with gods gave their protection to the names of courtiers, scribes, water-board officials and other worthies. However, while such designated commoners were allowed in the epic it was still not proper for them to enter the royal box.

DARIUS

DA	A	RA	YA	VA	U	SHA
#	*	*	#	#	#	#

Figure 2.5   An asterisk placed beneath a syllable sign denotes its vital signalling character, as is shown when it is tested in isolation. The lattice denotes a wide-extent, suppressive sign.

KLEOPATRA

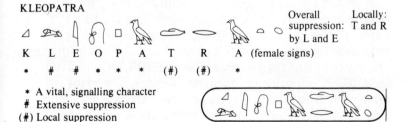

Overall suppression: by L and E
Locally: T and R

K	L	E	O	P	A	T	R	A (female signs)
*	#	#	*	*	*	(#)	(#)	*

* A vital, signalling character
# Extensive suppression
(#) Local suppression

Figure 2.6   Cartouche isolation of the pharaoh

Structurally, a cartouche is not an ellipse, which would ensure local suppression. A cartouche is formed by two arcs joined by parallel lines: this would normally be unsuppressed. In the horizontal position it must have the added upright line to obtain the local suppression. When upright the cartouche does not magnetically require a plinth-line, although it may have been aesthetically desirable.

3 Magnetic protection in nature

All seeds, whether of plant, insect or animal, are packed with the strongest concentration of nutriment that the parents' metabolism can provide. This endowment sustains the embryo from the first moment of independent life. In the case of plants this is the period from germination until its own external equipment for absorbing energy and nourishment comes into use through root development, leaf photo-synthesis, respiration, rain-stream direction and shade provision. The embryo emits a radiation signal of high intensity in keeping with its chemical concentrates which, were it not magnetically suppressed, would advertise it to countless, distant, co-resonating birds and herbivores, which would then be drawn to the plantation. But suppressive leaf-structures are already functioning even before a bud opens or the 'foliage' or first leaves unfold: in a plant's spring or summer maturity the leaves' inclined planes of suppression prevent the chemical betrayal of the future seed's concentrates while they are still being channelled to the flower trusses.

A plant's chemical signals are conducted along the arteries and veins of its leaves and issue from the tips and edges. The purpose of the plant's uniquely personal signal-links with its scattered seed is perhaps less obvious in the case of a rooted plant than in that of an animal which uses its shed debris as a guide on its home journeys. The plant remains in radiational correspondence with its seeds while they awaken through damp-soil action and warmth and begin to draw on the nutriment endowment until adequate root and leaf development is achieved. On the emancipation of a seedling the personal link between parent plant and seedling is discontinued. It cannot be renewed as the latter has now become a unique individual with its own personal oscillation rate.

Now, as I have suggested, the alignment of a suppressive sign at right angles across chemical links blocks the correspondence. The sculpted or coloured artery and veins in a leaf, which form the sign, are composed of identical chemicals which differ from those in the platform of the leaf on which they are mounted or depicted: chemical isolation of a sign's constituent parts from the platform is essential to its efficacy. Various arrangements of suppressive signs are produced by the leaves of different genera and species. Some sign-types afford wide-extent suppression such as those depicted in the South Spanish rock-art examples. Other types give local suppression. Judged by the present approximation method, the suppressive range of individual leaves of the bay-tree, *Lauris nobilis,* can vary between 35 cms and 40 cm, according to the size of the leaf and the fluctuations caused by the stimulating agent during the day and season. The stiffness of the bay-leaf maintains its rigid planes of suppression for some time after it has been plucked. It was probably this aspect which commended its use to Roman emperors when using wreath-protection against unwanted radiation from both celestial and mundane sources.

The feather-like sign-structure in a leaf can be repeated, thus extending the force-field coverage (Figure 2.7 (a) (b) and (c)). Further extension of this form is obtained when leaves are grouped around a stalk whose overall outline repeats the feather-form (Figure 2.7, (d) and (e)). Leaf-

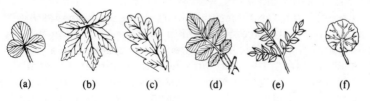

(a)   (b)   (c)   (d)   (e)   (f)

Figure 2.7   Leaf-signs and sign-forms

grouping in an overall trident-and-shaft effect (Figure 2.7, (a) and (e)), and twig-like signs (Figure 2.7 (f)), provide other variants of the basic feather form.

The Poseidon trident, Ψ , while suggested by twig and leaf-signs, may have been derived from a sea-bird's footprints in damp sand. This suppressive sign is shown, in prototype form, in the caves of Lascaux where it is placed in front of a bull's foot.

Other wide-extent leaf suppression occurs in linear and filiform types. While microscopic examination would, no doubt, disclose their artery and vein patterns, they seem to rely mainly on the curves which the leaves of these types assume. The curve and arch form very efficient and extensive suppressors, a universal sign which primitive man was swift to employ in his wooden wigwams for sanctuary use.

There is in nature another ubiquitous suppressive sign which gives magnetic protection to many plants and animals, confined to local areas of their structures but designed to inhibit radiative self-betrayal. This suppressive principle, which I have named the four-sector chord suppressor, occurs in many plant stalks, leaves and sepals, and on many fish, shell-molluscs, and in the body stripes on a zebra's rump for instance. In a curved surface a protective screen is formed across each four-unit sequence, so arranged that a fifth unit cannot intrude into and destroy the protection of the sign. In nature the units are separate stripes of chemical colour which differ in chemical content from the curved surface on which they appear. In man's protected buildings the air-separated contiguous pillars in a peristyle must be so arranged that each four pillars in a sequence must share the same vertical and horizontal planes so as to exclude a fifth unit (Figure 2.8). Fish and reptiles occasionally form four-sector chords from spots.

Free-standing architectural pillars (as at Stonehenge) are separated by air space. Sculpted or coloured bands on flowers and fish, being chemically different, are separated in a similar way from the body on which they appear. In plants the sign-separation on leaves and sepals is achieved by the chemically different stiffening ingredients of the raised 'ribs'. Four-sector chord, local suppression is used by the

Plantaginaceae such as the Hoary Plantain, *Plantago media*, and by many among the Liliaceae, such as Solomon's Seal, *Polygonatum multiflorum*.[8]

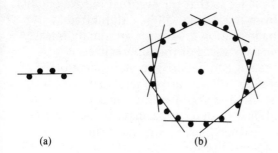

(a)   (b)

Figure 2.8   The four-sector chord suppressor. Each chord must intersect the outsides of points 1 and 4 and the insides of points 2 and 3

The arrangement of buds is, of course, essential for allowing free radiation of the flowers' chemical attraction at pollination time. Inflorescence has evolved along at least two different lines. First, as with plants of the flower-head or spike type, there are those which occupy a beacon-tower position well above the level of suppressive leaves. Yarrow affords a good example. The leaf sequences radiationally protect the stem during its channelling of nutriment to the bud which must still suppress the potential seed endowed with nutriment. Second, as with plants such as the Bay laurel and Acacia, inflorescence occurs within and below the levels of leaves, which must be so aligned as to allow the free flow of chemical broadcasts along the broad faces of their suppressive signs.

The strategy of plants which need pollination by winged insects is to entice a sufficient number from a distance but only at a time when the flowers are ready. Correct deployment thus relies on precise timing during optimum conditions of temperature and humidity and is intended to cover only the effective pollination period. This is to minimize exploratory damage which might otherwise be done if premature notification attracted untimely arrivals. The flower, when in tight bud or in the half-opened state, still inhibits the chemical broadcast from the stigma's

radiational beacon because the protective signs in sepals
and in petals, or in both, prevent its issue. In anticipation of
pollination time the flower buds protrude above or between
the suppressive leaf planes so that the eventual release of
beckoning signals from the stigma will be uninhibited in
most directions. The invitation broadcasts are finally released
through the bending backwards of the suppressive
planes of retracted sepals and petals. The multiplication of
suppressive sign defences in plant leaves, sepals and petals
is matched by birds, fish and shell-molluscs, many of which
appear to be second lines of defence against accident to the
primary defences of feathers, scales or spiral forms. In
addition, birds and fish utilize fortuitously the protection of
land, riverine and marine foliage, as did man's remote
ancestor and, later, proto-man in his arboreal situations.

The stigma and style seem to be the transmitting points of
chemical information. Paul Jaeger[9] states that Fitting, during
his orchid studies, showed that the stigma of a flower, when
chemically stimulated, transmits its reaction in such a way
as to control the whole perianth. As sepals and petals
incorporate suppressors and as some flowers appear before
a plant's leaves, Fitting's suggestion of a collateral line of
descent from a common plant ancestor, whose original
bud unit has since become divided, is supported by the
continuance of separate suppressive devices in sepal and
petal. Another employment of suppression is found in the
four-petalled Cruciferae, the sixteen-petalled chrysanthemum
and allied plants.

Ripe fruit and grain radiations must attract faunal
consumer-porters to their localities from afar so that seed
may be carried to fresh ground, there to be deposited with
the creature's initial endowment of fertilizer. Fauna, having
obtained nourishment from flora, must pay for that service
by returning the by-products of the body for soil
revitalization. Only modern man ignores this law of nature.
However, during its passage through a body, the seed-germ
must be protected from rapid dissolution by the creature's
digestive process. The plant has allowed for this by giving
the kernel a coat hard enough just to survive the known
period and yet be sufficiently softened — stone or pip — to

facilitate germination in the soil.

A twig, when stripped of its leaves, conforms with the familiar artery and vein pattern of suppression in certain alignments. Deciduous trees and shrubs thus appear to maintain some magnetic protection in their still obscure winter behaviour, possibly to avoid the distant radiational attraction of winged parasites.

Primitive man had constructed his protective artefacts from the visual sign suppressors encountered in nature. It is thus of great interest to find, through the microscope, that the cellular structure of living matter contains its own suppressive signs and alignments. For instance, the starch grains of maize, oats and wheat have suppressive sign-forms. Maize grains of hexagonal (unsuppressed) shape bear tetramorphic suppressive signs; those of oats carry the scale-interstice sign suppressor, as appears on fish and reptiles, and the wheat starch grain has disc form.[10] While their broad planes would be suppressed they would signal from their edges. Similarly, the epidermal hairs on young stems contain minute suppressive signs. In one example the background contains a mesh of scale-interstice signs overlaid by perfect Maltese crosses.[11]

The bird, in addition to its self-suppression by feathers, has benefited enormously by the tree's leaf and twig magnetic protection and the supply of leaves and small twigs to use in its radiationally insulated nest. The survival of naked chicks has been due largely to these factors as with the survival of myriads of other genera and species, including man. The Oven bird's mud hut contains a nest chamber which is internally protected with a spiral form and externally marked with serpentine or meander sign mud ridges which cover its dome. It is often sited so that a leafy branch overhangs the entrance. The Bower bird's shelter incorporates suppressive arches and lattice-crossings according to the positioning of the sticks or reeds used in its construction. The floor is also made of layers of crossed reeds, and is presumably suppressed against the attentions of burrowing rodents and insects. A tree trunk, of upright cylinder form, would give local suppression. Woodpeckers cut suppressive circular holes. Other tree-bole nesting species protect the entrances with dome-form mud, cemented with saliva which, applied externally, also provides the homing target. The Greater-Spotted woodpecker evolved large, white, pinnate-design suppression in addition to the normal feather protection of its tail. This may be protective insurance because when working on a hole, its beak's vector and receptor port is not free directionally to apprehend chemical warning signals.

The acute observation of the artist/writer, Roland Green[12] is of great assistance in our magnetic defensive context. Green says: 'Feathers . . . are in groups, confined to definite tracts . . . . Birds . . . are able to move any group of feathers independently and they can, by muscular action, depress or raise all their plumage.' This explains the extension of the magnetic-protective shields of the tail- and wing-spread of an alerted peacock, turkey, duck or hen. When a broody hen conceals very young chicks beneath her feathers it is not only to keep them warm or out of sight.

We find, by Revealer tests, that chemical interchange operates through a bird's beak, a fish's snout and the human thoracic area. The stretched-out neck of the bird which is chemically searching both on the ground and in homing flight, does not only balance its body. The beak is advanced well through the suppressive planes of neck and breast feathers, similar in effect to a flower's inflorescence protruding above leaf suppression. As the beak is the radiating point it must be suppressed, for self-protection, when the bird is sleeping or relaxing. This is done by tucking the beak beneath the suppressive planes of the feathers at the top of a wing. When sea-birds are relaxing in this way their legs are covered by the suppression of the scale-interstice signs that occur in fish and reptiles.

The chick, covered only in down, is magnetically unprotected and thus vulnerable to detection by distant predators until its feather defences are adequately formed. Roland Green comments on the feather deployment of a mallard duck when alarmed:[13] 'She has her tail spread and wings dropped as she leads the chicks away.' She has interposed herself and dropped her wings to extend the magnetic-protective screens of her plumage between the chicks and the chemically apprehended direction of danger.

Another of Green's illustrations shows the deployment of a duck's tail-feathers when on water. The tail is raised to cast a magnetic screen under which the chicks follow, thus being protected from overhead. Chicks in the rear stations accelerate when they sense that they have lagged beyond the protective aura of the tail-feathers' radiational umbrella.[14]

Sign-structures in nature which protect eggs offer archetypal hints useful in man's development of magnetic-protective architectural forms. While the external calcium carbonate in a bird's egg-shell can be instrumentally detected, the shell's form prevents the broadcast of chemical food concentrates present in the embryo. Half of a bird's egg-shell, when pressed gently into uncooked pastry, is shown to be a completely efficient local suppressor when an otherwise signalling item is placed within it. The architectural dome derives from this defensive property. The egg-sac of the *Zelotes latreillei* spider is protected by being covered with a circular 'barrow',[15] a device echoed by early man in his burial mounds. The suppression of veined leaves is used by the spider *Araneus cucurbitinus*[16] to give lateral and underside protection to its egg-sac's sanctuary. The spider bends the leaves to construct a rough inverted hollow cone and fixes it in position by the binding, magnetic-protective web placed over its top. Another species, *Philodromus histrio,* uses the suppressive force-fields of heather shoots to protect its egg-sac.[17] Fish eggs are placed in purses which are sign protected. The egg-purse of the Cat shark incorporates the four-sector chord device, as occurs in leaves of the plantain type; the Port Jackson shark's egg-purse is a spiral structure, and the embryo of the skate is placed within a domed case with tetramorphic ends.[18]

A spider's web-sign prevents chemical interflow through its locally suppressive area and vertical alignment. The successful deployment of this fly-trap seems to depend on the spider's sensorial ability to choose popular food-radiating routes along whose ray-paths winged insects will be drawn towards the pasturage targets. The spider interposes its web across a chosen, suitably resonating route. The winged insect, with its characteristic swerving flight, seems to be sampling the chemical content of several adjacent food-links and comparing their relative intensities. When, during such lateral swerves, the sudden incidence of a web's suppressive screen interrupts the guiding ray-path to which the insect is committed, the momentary bewilderment caused by this sudden loss of guiding signals distracts the insect's attention and it crashes into the net. The spider chooses a locally suppressive device because an extended force-field around the web would cause the insect to change course earlier and thus avoid it. Also the spider must periodically check the continuing attractiveness of the food-radiating route it is employing. It does this by moving out to the attachment points of the web where the local suppression ceases to operate.

Spiders can sink their bodies beneath the extensive suppressive planes of their four or eight bent knees. Most carry suppressive feather-type signs on their backs. During moulting some spiders make use of overhead suppressive crosses in the web from which they hang upside down.[19]

Flies, when their wings are crossed over their backs in the resting position, obtain extensive protection. The loss of the rigid planes of suppression due to rapid wing movements in flight may be a reason for protective signs on the backs of winged insects. The female of the Emperor moth[20] has very prominent protective signs. The wings have four spots, meander and twig signs, and its body has four-sector chord colour-banding; the four-sector chords operate when the body is curved slightly downwards. Butterflies' wings are similarly suppressed.

The eggs of moths and butterflies are usually laid on the undersides of leaves so that the emerging caterpillars can also enjoy their protective force-field cover. Eggs are self-suppressed by the dome form, often reinforced by four-sector chord 'ribs' or, as in the moths *Catocala concumbens, C. neogama* and *C. recta*,[21] by a sign-form closely resembling the spider's web pattern.

Caterpillars have protective signs on their bodies such as a raised lattice pattern, or bands or spots of colour which form four-sector chords when they curl up; the body segments also provide four-sector chords in the curled-up position. The chrysalis, which has four sector-chords formed

by its spiky edges in many species, is often attached to a
plant where it will obtain leaf protection.

When settled on a flower, leaf or sunny wall a butterfly's
most effective protective wing angle is slightly less than a
completely flat display position and rather more than 45°
from the closed-wings posture. The wing alignment of this
three-quarters open display produces oblique force-fields
similar to those of leaves on a single stem. The closed-wings
position gives extensive lateral protection to the butterfly
against being sensed from the sides. However, the insect can
still receive food signals from ahead or be detected by a
predator placed in front or behind it. The displaying butterfly
sometimes moves its feet to switch its direction. This seems
to be a response to its apprehension of a predator's searching
vector and which causes it to swivel and present its wing
suppression against that direction. Insects such as the Praying
Mantis and the Chinese Oak Silk moth have large, feather-
form antennae rising from their foreheads. Chemical
interchange seems to operate through the antennae edges
and tips. The broad surface sign-form gives extensive
protection to the insect across its front when the head is
tilted. Another insect, *Phyllium siccifolium*, known as the
Moving Leaf, has an imitation leaf-form on its back and thus
enjoys the protection of this sign against overhead chemical
detection. Camouflage is a visual last resort in attempts to
escape notice. The Butterfly fish also uses the leaf- or twig-
sign as a supplementary suppressor to its basic scale-sign
protection.

A fish, when tested with its head still on its body,
broadcasts its internal food chemicals. A sample was
extracted for Revealer matching. When the fish is decapitated
those internal chemicals can no longer be detected. The
snout or beak being the chemical interchange port, and the
fish being unable to shield its snout, as the bird does its beak,
it must retreat behind the magnetic protection afforded by
aquatic plants when it senses a predator's searching vector.
The scale form appears to be the first line of magnetic
defence. Further experiments with a decapitated herring,
from which the scales had been carefully removed, showed
that it is still suppressed. The interstice signs, between the

scales, are reproduced on the matrices which hold the scales. These provide suppression by a sign similar in form and identical in function to the elongated, four-limbed cross X which appears in Mesolithic South Spanish rock art. This basic protective sign occurs between the scales of turtles and tortoises, serpents and lizards, on birds' legs, in unopened carpellate fir-cones, the white spaces on a giraffe's coloured skin and in the dark markings of the reticulated giraffe, etc. It is also found at the junctions of hexagon cells in honeycombs and their grub breeding chambers.

Tests on the backbones of plaice, soles and flounders show that they cast extensive force-fields comparable with those of the arteries and veins of leaves of similar size. The fish-backbone sign was extensively depicted in Mesolithic rock art. It may furnish an extra line of defence against radiational betrayal of highly concentrated spawn chemicals in the organs below the backbone's horizontal level. The back of the mackerel carries coloured meander and chevron signs. The Rorqual whale has four-sector chords in ridges along its underbelly.[22] The Compass jelly-fish has sixteen spokes in its wheel sign overlying its dome form:[23] perhaps the four-multiple spokes operate when the creature is in its flat posture, just before the propulsion stroke, at a time when its dome is magnetically ineffective. Flat-fish frequent habitats without protective aquatic plants so they partly bury their heads in sand or silt. The radiating point then lies horizontally below the many angles of the scale-interstice protected signs owing to the slant of its body. The eyes protruding just above the sand surface may rely on globular or dome local suppression.

Many grass snakes appear to rely on two signs only; the serpentine shape and the scale-interstice signs. However, vipers such as *Natrix maura* also employ colour signs · superimposed over the scales. This viper goes through three colour-sign stages; the viperine, tesselated and the striped.[24] Of these stages the first produces the meander sign, the second an elongated cross sign and the third a four-sector chord suppression. The Horse-shoe snake has a boomerang or arch sign on its head, and spaced colour patches to provide four-sector chords when in a coiled position.[25] Other vipers use the zigzag meander sign formed by a diamond pattern sequence which is familiar in the adder. Kirkland's tree snake inflates its neck considerably when alarmed,[26] while the Indian grass snake[27] grossly extends its body when swallowing a frog. Both expand the meander sign along their bodies.

When a snake is at rest it can suppress its own radiation from overhead chemical detection by placing its signalling snout below the top levels of its coiled body. This effect is comparable with the bird's neutralized beak when it is tucked beneath the wing coverts. The forked form of a snake's tongue acts as the sending and receiving chemical-interchange antennae when it protrudes through its snout's frontal sign suppression. Referring to a viper's capacity to follow prey which it has struck only once, in order to avoid possible damage to itself, Steward writes: 'the most powerful venom does not immediately kill the prey, which may travel some distance before it succumbs.'[28] The viper's success in following its prey has been attributed to the sense of smell and the use of Jacobson's organ in conjunction with the snake's tongue.[29] However, as smell is only effective within very short range, where some distance is involved the viper follows its victim by personal chemical interchange. It uses its tongue antennae to 'home' into its own personal signal injected into the victim's body. This enables the viper to quickly identify and find the direction of the individual animal it has struck and thus marked out among all others of the same scent, type, etc.

The ability of grazing animals, such as the elk, to find their winter-fodder plants buried beneath a heavy snowfall is made possible by the non-suppressive, six-pointed hexagonal structure of water crystals. The many water crystals, photographed by the late W.A. Bentley under the microscope, plainly show this characteristic signalling form.[30]

The chemical by-product, colour, results from the selective absorption, refraction or reflection of the light-rays which strike specific chemicals in the impacted object. So chevrons, meanders, spots or bands of identical colours represent identical chemicals and are linked in defensive sign patterns. Cockle shells such as *Sunetta scripta* L. [31] and *Circe scripta* L. [32]

afford examples where the local suppression of the shell-form is reinforced with coloured signs. Local suppression is provided by the shell structure of limpet, mussel, cockle, scallop and other bi-valves. The mollusc *Turris babylonia* L. has sculpted and coloured four-sector chord arrangements superimposed on an already very efficient spiral-form suppression. Extensive magnetic protection is achieved through the spiral in the tower portions of a gasteropod's shell. This spiral extends its force-field to a considerable area, as indicated in Table 2.1.

TABLE 2.1

	Shell's diameter (cms)	Time	Suppressed radius (cms)	Time	Suppressed radius (cms)	Time	Suppressed radius (cms)
Whelk	4·0	09.00	24·0	17.30	25·0	22.50	25·9
Whelk	3·8	09.00	23·4	17.30	24·4	22.50	25·0
Whelk	3·2	09.10	22·1	17.35	23·1	22.45	23·7
Whelk	2·8	19.10	22·0	17.35	23·0	22.45	23·6
Dog-whelk	1·8	19.15	18·0	17.40	19·2	22.40	19·6
Dog-whelk	1·7	19.15	17·8	17.40	19·1	22.40	19·4

The widely extended magnetic protection spread by the spiral form of a gasteropod mollusc's shell protects it from above and at the sides by an 'umbrella' of horizontal and oblique suppressive planes. To allow the free working of its sensors which protrude through the defensive system, local suppression at the aperture is essential. The break in the near-circular circumference of the aperture's underside is restored to a circle's locally suppressive integrity by a 'returned-port' device (Figure 2.9). The arch-form suppression across the aperture end is pierced outwardly by the sensors. The returned-port form was so named or cited by Sir Cyril Fox, who found it architecturally employed at the entry/exit ports of some circular Welsh burial barrows (of which more later).

Thus the spiral-shelled gasteropod is only exposed to distant chemical detection by predators on or below the seabed when its sensors are extruded through the aperture during feeding, or when extending the building of its shell.

Figure 2.9   Spiral suppression in the whelk. Note the 'returned-
port' aperture

The eggs of *Cantharus macrospira berry* attach to the shell's
outside, in the pre-veliger stages, [33] and are then enclosed
within the shell's widely extended suppression.

Scallop shells of both *Clamys* and *Pecten* genera have been
widely valued as religious emblems since the Middle Ages
when *Pecten jacobaeus*, associated with St James of Santiago,
and *Pecten albicans*, a Mediterranean species, influenced
religious architecture and became a heraldic charge on the
coats of arms of pilgrim families. Sir Mortimer Wheeler, in
his survey of the scallop's religious associations, mentions
that the earliest known representation of the Birth of
Aphrodite from a scallop shell occurs in a Greek-made
artefact, dated approximately 400 BC, which was found at
Taman on the Black Sea.[34] Its active, religious, protective use
must antedate by many aeons the long transition from times
of sensorial appreciation of its magnetic virtue, through
legend, to this felicitous myth. Scallop suppression of the
intensive radiation of the embryonic Aphrodite before
achieving the nubile state is paralleled by the flower bud's
magnetic protection by sepal and petal until it is ready for
pollination.

Scallops which have been tested are *Pecten albicans* and
Pecten maximus, the latter being the large, edible mollusc
which renders experiments and close visual examination of
its shell relatively simple. The deep concavity of the lower or
left valve of *Pecten maximus* locally suppresses a radiating
sample placed within its hollow. The 'ribs' running down its
shell produce a series of four-sector chords. However, the
upper or right valve of this species is so shallow that the
near-flat curve of the large ribs cannot, of themselves,
provide the alignment demanded by four-sector chords. So
the creature developed fine, raised, striations which overlie
the large ribs and repeat, in miniature, the necessary align
alignment of four-sector chords (Figure 2.10). If a lower
valve of *Pecten maximus* is pressed down, edgeways, into a
strip of Plasticine, the fine, curved striations which this
valve also carries can be seen in the mould as well as the
imprints of the larger rib sectors. The Italian word for shell is
nicchio: hence the naming of the niche, usually of scallop-
shell design, which magnetically protects a saint's statue
placed within it.

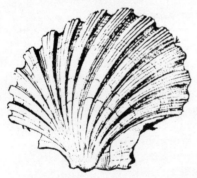

Figure 2.10 Primary and secondary ribs of four-sector chords on the
convolutions of a scallop

The Leaf-cutting ant of Mexico uses the leaf segments as
packing around its nest. This employment of the leaves'
suppressive signs ensures that the radiations from the queen
and larvae do not issue to attract distant predators. Eugène
Marais describes how *Eutermes* worker ants build arches. [35]

Apart from its mechanical strength the arch sign has extensive magnetic-suppressive capability of the kind we are discussing. The ants calculate both spacing and alignments of the arches so that their force-fields will overlap to give maximum coverage.

Marais also reports the encirclement of the queen in her cell by a number of soldier ants which are equally spaced from one another. The angle of the plane of this ant circle relative to the water level far beneath them, was about 45° and to accomplish this angle some soldier ants stood while some hung from the roof.[36] From our point of view, this exercise insulates the queen's secretions by protective circulation of chemicals through the soldier ants' bodies; the circle would also cover oblique angles unprotected during arch construction. An angle of 45° from ground level is the crucial one used in assessing the depth of an underground signalling source with the Revealer. Thus it seems the ant circle's angled plane of 45° could enable them to monitor the water level.

The force-field protection offered by leaf and feather explains why great virtue was attached to tree and bird in myth and legend. Derivatives are the sacred oaks, mistletoe, cherubim and vultures' wings. The latter were prominent in Pharaonic ritual. Ritual accessories such as eagle lecterns, acanthus leaves and evergreen decoration of churches at Christmas time proclaim their magnetic-protective functions. In the flood epic of Gilgamesh and in Genesis the return of God's protection is assured to Ut-Napishtim and Noah through the homing of raven and dove to the ark before the waters go down. The olive leaf, or branch, presages restored tree protection and peace to Noah and to all mankind, the promise to be ratified within the wide embrace of the covenanted rainbow.

The vertical seed-pod of the bulrush seems to be the natural archetype inspiring the exclusive Pharaonic cartouche. The legend of Moses being found in the flags (bulrushes) by Pharaoh's daughter seems to fuse the royal favour of his adoption with the origin of the cartouche.

Prehistoric knowledge of the physical containment of chemical radiation which would otherwise betray is exemplified in the screening effect of a spider's web and of birds' wings. This passed into legend as miraculous protection such as by angels. There is a Jewish legend concerning David hiding from Saul in a cave. The Targum relates David's prayer: 'I will pray before the most high God, who called a spider to weave a web for my sake in the mouth of the cave.'[37] During his flight from Mecca to Medina, the prophet Muhammad and his companions eluded the pursuing Koreish by hiding in a cave on Mount Thur, south-east of Mecca. A miracle saved them from detection. The searchers were deceived into thinking that the cave was untenanted as two doves had laid their eggs at the entrance which was also covered by a large spider's web.[38]

Architectural sanctuary

1 The structure of the sanctum

Man's cave-dwelling epoch, when magnetic-protective signs were first engraved or painted on the walls, foreshadowed the growth of the architectural sanctuary. In the regression from memory to legend, and from legend to myth, Mithras — the Western counterpart of the Persian god of light, Ahura Mazda — was born from the Rock. The prototype of his temples was that rocky cave of fact in which Aurignacian and Palaeolithic scientists had outwitted predatory beasts by chemically insulating themselves within their sanctuaries. The myth preserving that far-off intellectual victory over the great predatory beasts underlies the Mithraic ceremony. It culminated in the triumphant blood-offering of the vanquished Bull, the epitome of the force and threat of nature. The Mithraic cult persisted into the periods when flora had generally replaced fauna on the sacrificial altars.

The daily and seasonal chemical communications permeating the natural world had been fully used by early man and the physical controls of the phenomenon were understood from Aurignacian to Neolithic times. When the reflex-response to this sensory stimulus had generally faded the vaguely apprehended vibrations still experienced by seers and priests were erroneously intellectualized as the moods of various supernatural entities. Sun-god worship was soundly based, since all life and religions depend on the stimulus of cosmic radiation in which the sun plays a major part so far as our solar system is concerned.

Man's use of signs and ritual in fertility cults was rare compared with their employment in burial cults. Many signs have thus been erroneously attributed to fertility cults by anthropologists.

In addition to plant, fish and fowl, the edible shell-mollusc played a major part in formulating early man's interlocked artistic and scientific education. It provided a further working set of sign-form archetypes through which man extended the scope of his defensive essays in sanctuary construction. The limpet is archaeologically attested as being a very early staple item in the diet of primitive people who lived near the sea-shore. It was inevitable that the magnetic self-protection of this mollusc's shell construction would be recognized by people still responsive to chemical interchange sometime during its constant use as food. When, for instance, the limpet was held in a certain position its food signals would be interrupted. When the shell was crushed the contents would radiate the chemical signals.

The conception of the religious sanctum, germinating in the seed-bed of primitive man's mind, is without parallel in his evolution towards civilization. As the molluscs' protective architectural devices spawned the king-priest societies, so those societies in turn caused near atrophy of the chemical-interchange dimension within mankind's sensorial endowment. This functional loss enforced an enormous compensatory surge of intellectual development bringing with it the unreliability inherent in a newly acquired substitute 'organ'. Intellect, based on sensory responses lacking the vital corroboration of radiational cross-checks, was always liable to error when attempting to make other sensory impressions fit into an overall significance. The full endowment of co-ordinated reflex-senses was as instantly reliable and efficient in early man as in other fauna.

Pythagorean and Jungian philosophy have drawn attention

to an indefinable quality attaching to the tetraktys, or rule of four. Let us refer directly to Jung in this respect: 'Surveying these facts as a whole, we come, at least in my opinion, to the inescapable conclusion that there is some psychic element present which expresses itself through the quaternity.'[1] He continues, referring to the mandala: 'It is therefore more probable that we are dealing with an *a priori* "type", an archetype which is inherent in the collective unconscious and thus beyond individual birth and death.'[2]

Because of the lasting effect of their transferred physical power on the psyche, the cross, tetramorph and their four-multiples were, and continue to be, the greatest influences in the development and sustenance of modern religion, its ritual and architecture.

Certain limpet species construct dual-purpose defensive redoubts in soft rock to which they unerringly return after their food forays.[3] The redoubt's walls, banked and moulded accurately to the outer shell contours, act both as a breakwater and a suppressive 'barrow' precinct. The limpet, through its personal signal's homing vector, resonates with the excretions it used to concrete the outer rim of the oval bank. These signals guide the creature's return to its own redoubt. This limpet construction could have inspired the tentative efforts in the banked and ditched, circular or oval, precincts which man began to erect around his burials.

The limpet's dome affords local suppression within its perimeter. It appears to have been an archetypal model from' which the roofing of vernacular huts, the domes of ancient Greek Tholoi, the roof of the Temple of Vesta, and cathedral domes were evolved. No doubt the half egg-shell also influenced dome construction, such as in the igloo, for the same protective reason.

The gouged-out circular bases of the Bronze Age barrows, intended to prevent the reception of emissions from below those suppressive planes, afforded defence against the power of the chthonic Mother-goddess. The excavations directed by Sir Cyril Fox, and his cogent observations concerning a point of ritual,[4] indicate that communication between goddess and priest was conducted through a divine centre-point ⊙, a bothros hole cut through the protective horizontal planes of the circular ground form. The bothros was sealed with a suppressive clay dome which closed it aurally, visually and magnetically when not in use. Communication could only be initiated by the priest who removed the dome and later remade the seal, thus ensuring that no evil underworld influence would interfere with the interment. Sir Cyril wrote that in another type of barrow a mortuary hut had occupied the centre of the sanctum. Perhaps a dome-like, circular, holed roof, similar in form to a Keyhole limpet's shell with its central vent, was the type of roofing in secular use during that period.

The entry or exit ports in the outer wall of those excavated barrows had their openings 'returned', the term Sir Cyril used to explain the building outwards of the walls at those points which continued at the same levels and in the ground plan. This architectural feature maintains vertical protection by the horizontal planes down the height of the cylinder-form wall which would otherwise be lost if the breaks were un-returned (Figure 3.1). Of course, if there were four un-returned breaks in the circular form the suppression would be maintained. Concerning his excavations at 'Sheeplays 393',[5] Sir Cyril reported a second un-returned port in the circle. In view of the magnetic requirement of returned ports, one may doubt if that second opening was strictly contemporary with the otherwise protected barrow.

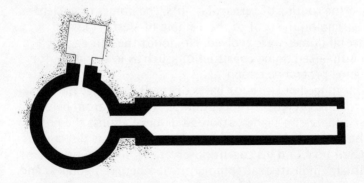

Figure 3.1 Plan of the Treasury of Atreus, showing two returned ports

Many old country churches, dating from Norman times, when viewed from the air disclose the circular or oval barrow precincts on which they were erected. An interment is the absolute pre-requisite for a religious foundation which, being known as such to the inhabitants, demanded the erection of a new edifice on the already holy ground.

Standing-stone or post circles have given rise to much speculation as to their purpose. Some such circles in West Cornwall have had fanciful origins attributed to them. Most carry moral warnings concerning people being changed into stone if such wickedness as gathering firewood or dancing on Sundays is indulged in. Few such stone circles have been preserved in their pristine completeness. If the number of stones which formerly stood can be accurately counted and measured in alignment from the centre, then the functional type and its ritual purpose can be more reliably ascertained. If there were, say, fifteen stones or posts in the peristyle and one in the centre, four-multiple overhead and underground magnetic protection would be assured. If there were sixteen units in the peristyle the whole enclosure would remain insulated above and below irrespective of any other stones within the enclosure. Small circles with vital numbers of stones in the peristyle, such as seven or nine, would be unsuppressed and might be used for supplication ceremonies. Large unsuppressed stone circles may have been used as moots where secular policy was discussed.

I set up experiments on the supposition that a stone or post circle must have some radiational, protective screen even when there seemed to be no obvious features that could provide the lateral insulation of the sanctuary within the peristyle. A simple model consisting of match-sticks pressed into a circular Plasticine base was arranged, and re-arranged, until a precise placing and spacing of the sticks resulted in a magnetic shield of local coverage. It was only when this was exactly achieved that the chemical correspondence between the tested items ceased. It was known that four sticks of the same chemical composition, when placed in line and sharing horizontal and vertical planes, provided a suppressive shield. The problem which a long-forgotten priest-architect had solved was how to maintain these jointly shared planes when the four units had to follow a curve. An explanation follows.

Tetramorphic lateral suppression was secured when any four (*only*) contiguous stones or posts formed a circumferential chord wherein the outer surfaces of posts 1 and 4 overlapped and shared the plane of the inner surfaces of posts 2 and 3 (Figure 2.8). This alignment was continued around the peristyle. Its success depended on the accurate spacing, cross-sectional thickness and placing of the posts in relation to the centre of the sanctuary. Stones were tooled and smoothed on the inward-looking faces if necessary, as with the sarsen peristyle at Stonehenge, so that no protuberance on a fifth stone, contiguous with a four-stone chord, allowed it to intrude into — and thus destroy — the protective tetramorphic facet. After testing many models I found this principle to be still operating with the contiguous four-group of sarsen peristyle stones still standing at Stonehenge in June 1972. Four-sector chords originally provided complete local protection around the peristyle (Figure 3.2).

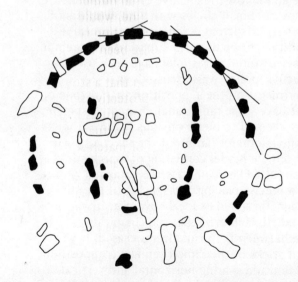

Figure 3.2   Peristyle of four-sector chords (Stonehenge)

Since thirty posts or stones, such as were in Stonehenge's peristyle, do not provide overhead or underground protection a stone-jointed, continuous circle ran along the tops of the sarsen pillars. When the number of stones in a peristyle form a multiple of four then overhead and underground insulation is assured up to the height, and down to the foot, of the shortest member. One to three extra stones included in the four-multiple peristyle would destroy that vertical protection: however, an extra holy stone placed well within the peristyle and not being incorporated in the magnetic flow around it does not destroy its overhead or underground insulation.

Stonehenge is a temple, probably dedicated to a god or goddess of measurement similar to the Egyptian goddess Sheshat who preceded Thoth in this office. Sheshat assisted the Pharaoh in 'stretching the cord' for measuring and marking out the size of a new temple.[6] Underground protection of the earliest precinct was the first suppressive measure undertaken, as the Mother-goddess seems to be the earliest conception of a supernatural being. This was executed by digging out a surrounding ditch and banking it with the soil. The entry and exit port(s) were also ditched and banked to continue the levels and provide the 'returned-port' feature to maintain the overhead and underground protection of the circle plan.[7] Professor Atkinson says: 'There were fifty-six Aubrey holes set in an accurate circle 288ft. in diameter, immediately within the inner margin of the bank.'[8] The four-multiple of Aubrey holes, which show no archaeological evidence of ever having carried poles or standing stones, could, in theory, supply underground insulation for the unsuppressed number of pillars in the blue-stone and sarsen circles. If, however, the Aubrey holes were the repositories of incinerated human remains, such contents would be contained within the magnetic flow around that multiple of four units and thus be protected from underground and overhead.

The trilithons at Stonehenge total a vital number, five, and are arranged in a segmented horseshoe sign within the sarsen peristyle. Whether or not there was an altar stone the area remains open to celestial communication as the trilithons pierce the overhead planes of the circular stone shield.

This links them with the sky-god whose radiations could then interchange with the trilithons' unsuppressed lintel tops on which an offering might be placed unless there was a protruding altar stone. The god's radiance travelled right down the trilithons' legs into the blessed area within those stones, being conducted through the stone circle's suppressive horizontal planes. As the priest-architect deeply respected the god's high energy potential, manifest in storms, he would hope to prevent dangerous radiation leaking from the trilithons' fronts, backs and sides. This could be effected, theoretically, through the suppressive Greek pi sign-form of their elevations, and by the solid tetragon figure of lintel ends and sides on the upright members.

Figure 3.3   Plan of Borobudur

The ancient Indian temple of Borobudur has many lines of magnetic defence (Figure 3.3). The central spire is vital and thus conducts interchange between the god and the altar. The central dome, with its protruding spire, is not included in the four-multiple vertical protection of the first circular precinct which is accomplished at a lower level by sixteen small-spired domes. Each succeeding circular precinct is a vertically protected four-multiple of domes and all have lateral protection by four-sector chords operating across their outsides. All the surrounding terraces have twenty facet wall-plans for vertical protection and their crenelated tops give lateral protection through the meander or dog-toothed sign. The four steps at ground level, one set on each side of the precinct, give extra tetramorphic protection from emissions below.

The rainbow, God's convenant with Noah, assured mankind's future protection. This seems to be one of the most obvious archetypes to inspire man's employment of this sign-structure as an architectural protector. The Egyptian goddess, Nut, is usually depicted giving the protection of her arched body when holding up the skies. Possibly, chemically sensitive primitive man recognized its protective function in the ribbed arches across the breadth of cowrie shells, the Bower bird's constructions and in the termitaries of the White ants.

2 Vernacular architecture

The typical Algonquin wigwam framework incorporates the protective signs of arch and circle which, where they meet and cross, provide extra oblique planes of suppression to give complete overhead and lateral protection. Four arches can be arranged in series, with four more placed at right-angles to the first series. Thus sixteen arch ends, when driven into the ground, assure the underground suppression of the floor. Where the horizontal circles are broken to form the entrance, the broken ends must just overlap the uprights of the two inner arches enough to form extended crossings at those points. This device suppresses the entrance (Figure 3.4).

Figure 3.4   Wigwam

The magnetic protection of a tepee, while different in principle, is very easily achieved. The method described here has been well tested in models large enough to chemically insulate a dog placed within the framework. The requirement is a four-multiple number of poles in the peristyle but bunched at their tops. This precise arrangement adds lateral and oblique angles of protection to the overhead and underground insulation provided by four-multiple standing poles; the occupants now enjoy omni-directional magnetic protection. Further experiment showed the same omni-directional protection is achieved if, say, fifteen poles are in the peristyle — or one less than a four-multiple — with a central pole also included in the top bunching (Figure 3.5).

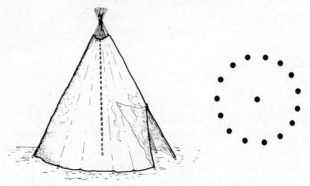

Figure 3.5   Tepee, additional experiment

The buildings of the Navajo indians, described by Amos Rapoport,[9] show a preference for the hogan log-hut. I have tested this form in two models, one square in plan and the other hexagonal. The results show that it is essential that the logs' protruding ends make four-multiples on each corner of the building to give wide-ranging lateral protection across them (Figure 3.6). Both models were completely insulated laterally, and the protruding four logs in the plan of the square one also gave vertical protection. With full-sized hogan huts, built on the chemically suppressed principle encountered in other vernacular architecture, four-sector chords would form across the rounded outsides of the four-multiple logs on every side and across the protruding log-ends at the corners. Twelve tiers of logs would lengthen the vertical axis of force-fields. The log-ends flanking the door jambs would be so placed as to ensure that their overlapping force-fields covered the entrance. Although four- or eight-sided hogans would be vertically protected, six-sided hogans would need a roof held on crossed rafters, perhaps resting on four posts sunk well into the ground.

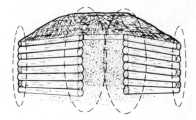

Figure 3.6   Hogan force-fields

The construction of the domed Zulu hut has been described by Biermann: 'In a foundation trench saplings are planted in a double row inclined in opposite directions laterally so that they criss-cross; about one metre above ground their tops are bent over and lashed together to form a series of interlaced arches in the plane of the wall.'[10] Those suppressive arches and their crossing-points would effectively shield the occupants from external chemical detection. The overlaid netting, which holds down the roof's reed-thatch, uses the locally suppressive sign-form of the spider's web. The web-like net should be made of woven grasses containing a different chemical ingredient from the thatch on which it rests. Sometimes a similar grass-woven frieze of saltire crosses is placed just below the dome top as a magnetic-protective embellishment. Biermann continues: 'Where the construction allows the thatch to be gathered in a finial, great care is lavished on its finish and decoration.'[11] The finial on the top of the dome may carry four uprights giving extended tetramorphic vertical protection. This Zulu structure is reminiscent of the dome of St Paul's Cathedral. The insulation of the entrance of the Zulu circular hut relies on the plaited-grass porch which, by protruding outwards, provides a returned-port device and restores the suppressive plan-design of the otherwise broken circle; its arch also provides extensive lateral protection. A composite drawing shows various external features (Figure 3.7).

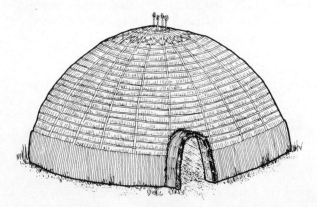

Figure 3.7   Zulu hut: Top, abafana, saltire crosses, spider's web thatch container. Woven porch gives returned-port circle plan continuance

Whereas the Zulu hut retains its physical detachment from each of its other self-insulated neighbours within the perimeter of the kraal, the Nabdam compound (Figure 3.8) shows a more sophisticated, patriarchal arrangement. Tests made on a graphite drawing of this compound plan confirmed the overall vertical insulation of the complete figure. The terminal sign $\_o o'$ at the compound's entry and exit port is similar in suppressive effect to the more usually encountered return-port device shown in the individual hut plans. In elevation these latter are protruding arches — as with the Zulu huts — laterally guarding the doorway of each unit in the perimeter-linked huts, all of which are already protected within the compound's continuous barrow-like wall. It seems possible that the protruding arch is a means of securing individual chemical privacy through withdrawal from community pressures that are chemico-emotively experienced in the living yard or club. One day it may be possible to determine, by experimental means, if a temporary metabolic change in glandular chemistry, brought about by heightened emotional intensity, may stimulate the same reaction dormant in a potential adversary by means of chemical interchange.

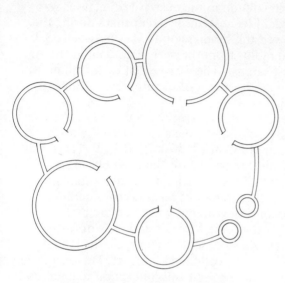

Figure 3.8   Nabdam compound, North Ghana, showing protected
perimeter

3 Temples of the ancient world

In the Azilian painted pebble ⊙, the continuous circle of the meander sign must be of the same material, paint in this case. The significance of this sign was realized during experiments with a limpet shell. First, the limpet was tested and was shown to be locally suppressed within the perimeter of the dome. With the dome cut off, the shallow skirting remaining around the base showed wide-extent suppression. Other tests were made on slabs of Plasticine from which the cogwheel sign-form was cut, first with a knife-point and then with a fluted pastry-cutter. This produced flutes and arrises similar to those which run down the columns of Doric, Ionic,

Corinthian and Composite Orders. Next a model of the circular columns of the Temple of Vesta at Tivoli was made.[12] The eighteen columns were simulated with internally stiffened sections of ribbed garden hose. The radius of protection which extended from each column in the outwards directions was extraordinarily wide. Five tests at different times during the day and night showed the suppression to vary between 35·1 cm and 38·1 cm in radius from the nearest column in the peristyle to the test sample. The diameter of each column was 1·5 cm. The archetype for the roof of this temple seems to have been the limpet shell.

Sir Banister Fletcher draws attention to the very early use of fluted and arrised columns at the entrance to the rock-tombs at Beni Hasan in Egypt (2130-1785 BC). [13] There may have been a mechanical necessity for the close placing of Greek temple columns for supporting the heavy entablature and roof. However, the paramount religious consideration governing this closeness of columns was to ensure that the overlapping range of the force-fields of each pair of fluted and arrised columns was sufficient to complete the lateral insulation of a rectangular, columned precinct. The architects of the Greek temples were to put this innovation to good use. Hitherto, lateral magnetic protection of rectangular peristyles had depended on the four-multiple system of plain columns in line across sides and ends. This had derived from the early huts with four posts presented on each side. The adoption of flutes and arrises on columns permitted variation of the numbers of columns, resulting in better proportion and balance in the design of the peristyle. The force-fields of neighbouring columns merged and overlapped, giving cover which now extended well beyond the visible external limits of the columns and into the precinct of the edifice.

The flute and arris sign-forms of the Azilian pebble proved to be very tolerant of damage. When an arris became chipped the magnetic flow around the column continued unabated as, being conducted by the continuity of the like-chemicals in the composition, it still followed the circular flow. While considerable overhead protection of a precinct was effected by the merging horizontal force-fields surrounding the tops of the flute-and-arris columns, the naos, or inner sanctum, was individually protected by the sign-form of its walls. Four pillars usually terminated the open ends of the long side walls of a naos and gave tetramorphic vertical protection to all within the sanctum irrespective of internal partition walls. The Greek letter H — *hieros* — protected the priest's title and originated in Phoenician script where it had two or three internal partitions. Both script versions are akin to the plans of a naos and bestow the same magnetic protection. The walls of the naos resting on foundations of the same sign would continue the suppressive layers below the dais on which the effigy was raised and protect the area from chthonic competition or intrusion into the sanctum.

In the large Greek temples of rectangular plan an internal, secondary peristyle was frequently incorporated. The flutes and arrises on such secondary columns extended the overlapping horizontal force-fields to reinforce overhead protection of the area between the outer peristyle and the naos walls. The inner peristyle often carried smaller, superimposed fluted columns. These, by extending the height of the lateral protection just above the raised effigies' levels, protected them on every side. The horizontal force-fields, by merging to give overhead cover for the celebrants, seem to have made additional roof suppression redundant, although the correct siting of acroteria on the ridges and corners of some gabled-roofed temples could add extra horizontal or oblique planes of overhead suppression.

Altars were originally placed in the open air and, lighted by the sun, gave direct contact with that god. However, when a holy relic or god-effigy was placed within a fully suppressed sanctuary it was withdrawn from radiational intercourse outside the building. This suggests its impounding as the chief asset of a community — so that its priests and the populace retained the exclusive benefit of its guarded aura of sanctity. Such shrine exclusiveness had to be relaxed in god-effigy temples.

Ruined temples, such as those of ancient Egypt and Greece, give rise to some speculation about details in their construction, and opinions vary considerably concerning the probable illumination of the Parthenon. Fletcher says that Fergusson suggested a clerestory, [14] Bötticher a sky-light, [15] while others suggested a wooden, ornamental roof. Either clerestory or sky-light, correctly orientated, could ensure the radiational purpose of this temple's upper storey. The sun's rays would directly light the effigy of Athena through either a rectangular, non-suppressed clerestory or an equivalent sky-light, thus allowing the effigy to be bathed in undiluted solar radiation on all its frequencies. The sun-god's local deputy, Athena, acted in liaison between god and priests. Apollo's effigy in his temple at Bassae 'was lighted from a large opening in the eastern side wall'.[16] In this latter case Apollo's effigy was treated as a personal 'relay' linking sun-god and officiants. The congregations, placed within the suppressed areas of temples, would be protected from the effects of a capricious god's 'displeasure', probably conveyed by dangerous radiation frequencies.

Dr George Crile, an eminent American surgeon, believed that 'Ultra-violet radiation plays the most prominent rôle in the body as it has the greatest power of generating electricity.'[17] Flora and fauna originated in a clearer, dust-free atmosphere which offered less filtering resistance to harmful celestial radiation than obtains in our times owing to our polluted atmosphere. In the periods when the conscious use of physical sign-protection was fading from the mind of urban man, the dim memories of the baneful effects of too much ultraviolet radiation may have persisted. This was rationalized as fear of 'the wrath of God', against which certain sign-forms, copied from nature, still protected him. As the attracting broadcasts of plants and the searching vectors of birds, fish, shell-molluscs and horned animals may be made within the ultraviolet regions of the spectrum, the apprehension of damage to living cells associated with over-absorption of ultraviolet wavelengths would be an added reason for the development of cosmic-radiation inhibitors which are also the magnetic-protective signs. As plankton is too minute to afford game for chemically sensing sea-birds, the vertical suppression evinced by a diatom's four-multiple rayed sign when it floats on the sea-surface may possibly have been evolved for this radiation-filtering purpose.

The temples with circular peristyles, like the Home of the Oracle at Delphi and the Temple of Vesta at Tivoli, have fluted columns which are also correctly spaced and positioned to conform with the lateral specifications of the four-sector chord. The extending of suppression through flutes and arrises seems, at first glance, superfluous. But as temples are primarily sanctuaries and may be functional in both structure and ornament we must look further. For a fugitive the physical aura of protection was now widely extended well beyond the outside of the temenos, the ground surrounding the temple. He had only to grasp a column to be quite sure that he was well within the sacred, invisible and protective mantle. In fact he would have enjoyed magnetic protection when he was within about 1·25 m from any column.

Tests on the model of the Temple of Vesta showed quite clearly that the flute-and-arris device made the plain-columned, four-sector chord method redundant. Removal of one plain column from the peristyle would have left a gap in that part of the temple's lateral defence. However, if a fluted and arrised column were removed the extensive force-fields around the adjacent columns adequately maintained the insulation. Why, then, did the priests take such care in maintaining the old alignments once the flute and arris made the alignments less critical? Evolution is gradual modification. The human appendix has only shrunk, it has not yet disappeared. Priestly architects, having used the circle and four-sector chord methods for so long, built on it rather than abandoned it. Perhaps, also, there was an element of insurance, which in fauna and flora appears to favour duplication of magnetic defences. In more recent times, steam-propelled vehicles were first known as horseless carriages, and retained the basic design of a vehicle which had remained virtually unaltered for thousands of years.

The pi sign-form, Π, is a suppressive device employed in Egyptian pylon temple entrances: the tetragon form is present, in section, in the more ancient Mastaba tombs.[18] The pyramid of King Zoser at Sakkara[19] is protected by the suppressive tiers of the tetragon form, which also produced meander step-edges along the corners. This latter feature is common in American Indian art. The pyramid of Cheops[20] exhibits some subtlety in its magnetic protection. At first glance it would seem to be a triangular-faced signalling unit. However, while the plaster outer casing presents triangular facets, the inner mass, being of different chemical compositon, is thus chemically separated from the casing material. Owing to the flattening of the inner material's apex, it produces tetragonal facets which afford the tomb's protection.

Experiments with a radiating sample inserted into the tomb area of a Plasticine Cheops-type pyramid show that interchange with the outside world obtains when the pointed apex produces triangular facets, and that suppression of the internal radiating sample occurs when the apex is flattened and the pyramid's edges slightly rounded. This protection only extends down to the pyramid's base, which accounts for the elevated positions of the tombs.

A similar slight rounding of edges is shown in the suppressed pyramid at Chichen Itzá,[21] and in the pyramid at Uaxactún. Projecting stairs and balusters, in cruciform, extend the plan's suppression. An open area on the platform allows radiation from sacrificial offerings to rise.

4 The quincunx

The arrangement of five items in a quincunx appears frequently in religious myth, ornament and architecture. Its function in representing a holy centre protected by four corner guardians has been observed by Jung:[22]

> Just as the stupas preserve relics of the Buddha in their innermost sanctuary so in the interior of the Lamaic quadrangle, and again in the Chinese earth-square, there is a Holy of Holies with its magical agent, the cosmic source of energy, be it the god Shiva, the Buddha, a Bodhisattva or a great teacher. In China it is Ch'ien — heaven — with the four cosmic effluences radiating from it.

Jung continues:[23]

> Among the various characteristics of the centre the one that struck me from the beginning was the phenomenon of the quaternity . . . there is often a competition between four and three. There is also, but more rarely, a competition between four and five . . . .

In our context it is a competition of force-fields. As a quadrangle and an earth-square are signalling signs in our present study, they cannot give magnetic protection as square or oblong figures. Jung's hint of competition between four and five stimulated me into further experimental activity.

The familiar aspect of the quincunx is the one-plane presentation •.• . As the force-field extending around four units in one plane appears to be circular, the interchange between five items would thus seem to produce lines of force

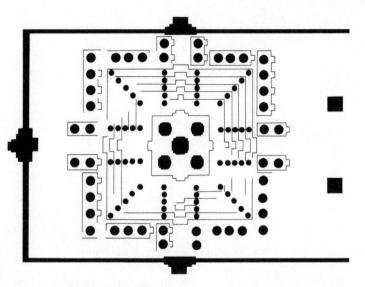

Figure 3.9   Plan of Bakheng

as embodied in the plan of the Temple of Bakheng (Figure 3.9). With rare insight Philip Rawson comments on this temple plan: 'The multiple towers of this shrine were meant to illustrate a mystical concept of the cosmos.'[24] In our present terms, the small towers running down in tiers from the top of the quincunx Holy Centre seem to flow out like radii. It will also be noticed that the outlying separate blocks of towers all combine in four-multiple suppression.

Experiments were made with five lumps of Plasticine mounted on a board in quincunx pattern. The test was to see

83

what would happen with a two-level quincunx. When the fifth and central unit of Plasticine was raised on a stick of different material, the effect was a change from extensive to local suppression. However, the suppressive 'edges' of this radiational pyramid continued down through the base units for a considerable distance. The realignment of the force-field is suggested in Figure 3.10.

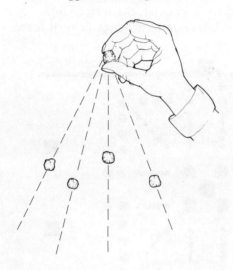

Figure 3.10 Theoretical force-field of two-level quincunx

A model was made to measure the penetrative range of the radiational pyramid beyond the base units. Results obtained with this model are set out in Table 3.1.

TABLE 3.1

Time	Four-unit base area	Fifth unit's height	Suppressive depth below
12.30	8 x 8 cms	5.5 cms	24.3 cms
16.10	8 x 8 cms	5.5 cms	24.7 cms
17.10	12 x 12 cms	15.0 cms	34.5 cms

This important magnetic-protective device with its great depth coverage is, in magnetic terms, an improvement on the more durable, but tremendously costly, solid pyramid. With the radiational pyramid the coverage of the interment can be much more simply effected.

The South Russian timber grave, c. 2000 BC (Figure 3.11),[25] is a classic example of the quincunxial pyramid's application. The upright posture of the suppressive horns on the skulls would allow the chemical interchange to operate as follows. The top skull's nose interchanges with the lower, front skulls' necks, and the top skull's neck interchanges with the lower, rear skulls' noses. The penetrating radiational pyramid thus formed protects the timber grave completely to a depth below its interment. The timber-grave building, being square, does not appear to have any other architectural suppression unless, perhaps, some logs overlying the interment formed a four-multiple. When constructing the quincunx the priest-architect would have known, precisely, the required height and spacing of the five skulls to ensure the penetrative protection.

Figure 3.11 South Russian timber grave

Tests with pointed lumps of Plasticine placed in the same quincunxial, two-level relationship produced the same radiational pyramidal effect. The quincunx device is often found on the steeples of English parish churches. A stone topping-collar is placed immediately below the spire's metal finial. This collar forms the top unit of the quincunx and interchanges with chemicals of the same stone in the four base pinnacles which surround the steeple. In such a radiational pyramid the body of the steeple between the upper and lower quincunx units must be of different chemical composition from them. This section is often made of wood and slate. Vertical crosses, used as finials on the base pinnacles, must cast their thin but extensive fields of suppression vertically, like the vertically placed horns in the timber grave, so as not to interfere with the chemical interchange between the topping-collar and the inner sides of the base pinnacles. If no quincunx was in operation, the four base pinnacles would form horizontal layers of wide-extent suppression. The pyramid appears to compress those force-fields within its own magnetic flow. The gain is in the depth of penetration of the local suppression extending downward to the lower levels of the tower.

Externally, the Taj Mahal (Figure 3.12) is a perfect example of the protection afforded by a radiational pyramid. As the finials on the main and subsidiary domes would have been made of the same rust-resisting material, a primary two-level quincunx is formed between them. If the finials on top of the four surrounding minarets are also of the same material, then a secondary radiational pyramid is also formed between them and the finial on the central dome.

The octagonal, horizontal sections of a church steeple, made of a uniform material, give local protection around top and sides. Dormers or effigies in the same stone applied to the slopes of the steeple provide tetramorphic layers of extensive horizontal suppression at those points (Figure 3.13). Similarly the base pinnacles repeat horizontally aligned extensive suppression down their lengths. Crockets, hook-like appendages applied around and down the sides of a steeple, also produce suppressive horizontal planes. Inside cathedrals transept piers have horizontal cross-sections in four-multiples.

Figure 3.12 Quincunx radiational pyramids of Taj Mahal

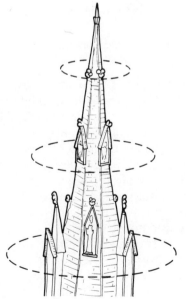

Figure 3.13 Tetramorphic vertical protection

Experiments have shown that no signals are received from the metal of a strip containing four or eight holes in a line. A strip with signalling numbers of holes does signal its chemical content: so a hole behaves in the same way as a dot (see Figure 2.3 columns 1 and 3). This experimental discovery explains the effectiveness of spatial signs — the form of hollow places, or negative space, in a building — which can also give protection. The cruciform shaft-tombs at Hua Chia Chuang, near An-yang, Honan Province, in China, are examples of this form (Figure 3.14).

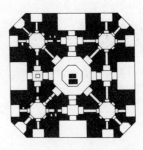

Figure 3.14 Chinese shaft-tombs

Figure 3.15 Plan of Taj Mahal mausoleum

The Gravettian 'Venus' (Figure 2.2) shows the spatial cross suppressor ✕. The plan of the Taj Mahal mausoleum (Figure 3.15) shows very sophisticated spatial-sign protection of the shrine. From the octamorphs of space around the centrally placed octagon tomb four corridors radiate to join with four octamorphic star spaces. Each star is also linked by passages to the four-limbed spatial areas. The truncated passages in each of the limbs of the octamorphic stars are of especial interest. They had to be added to complete the octamorphic spatial suppression, although they lead nowhere.

To the Western eye the distinctive feature of a Chinese or Japanese sacred edifice is the four upturned corners of its roof. This system gives horizontal layers of suppression across those points. The Great Shrine of Izumo, Japan (Figure 3.16), shows other interesting features which contribute to the overall magnetic defence of this Shinto example. These are the Chigy and the Katsuogi, whose names indicate their sanctuary connotations. The Chigy are the large wooden crosses formed by poles set astride the ridge pole, which give horizontal suppression across their four or four-multiple top ends. Also, each cruciform produces an upright suppressive force-field which prevents horizontal chemical correspondence. If, as seems likely, the Chigy poles were formerly continued into the ground, then apart from helping to stabilize the roof their extended force-fields would form protective radiational bulkheads within the shrine to protect the inner sanctum from end-on external influences. If those poles on either side of the shrine were composed of four or four-multiples then the lateral protection of the edifice would be assured.

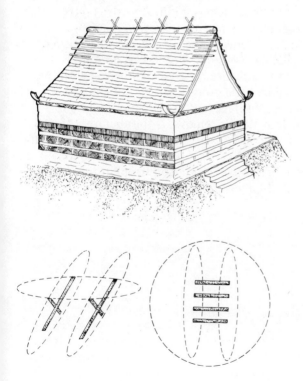

Figure 3.16 Shinto shrine with protective sign-form system

The Katsuogi are the groups of four log-like attachments placed below the ridge pole on both sides of the roof ends: they would provide tetramorphic planes of suppression along their lengths and across their butt-ends. The ends of the ridge pole usually carried either a suppressive sign such as a circle, or was of tetragonal cross-section, and this self-suppression would isolate it from the magnetic fields formed across the ends of each set of four-log units. The ridge pole and Katsuogi must be made of different material. A lattice fence around the precinct would give extra lateral protection to cover lower levels, and the curved gable-ends of the roof would reinforce the end protection of the shrine. It is also likely that some internal sign devices were employed as further insurance.

Religious ceremony and ritual survive mainly because of the use of symbols which represent their potent-sign originals in the recesses of the unconscious mind. Another factor which maintains the ritual continuance of forgotten magnetic protection, through symbols, is the devoted conservatism of the clergy over millenia. To them, and to certain quasi-religious societies, the ultimate heresy is tampering with the set ritual. There can be little doubt that the subconscious echoes of the feeling of safety and peace which the signs evoke, even in their symbolic remove, is the therapy offered by ritual. This is of increasing value as the stresses of unnatural life accumulate. Those who advocate the indiscriminate abandonment of religious ceremony and ritual in this present stage of human development know not what they do.

4

Chemical secrets of ceremony

1 The theriomorphic or animal gods

The earliest cults seem to have crystallized around
theriomorphic gods which transfigured the snake and the
bull, the thunderbird, the fish and the lamb. Their vestiges
have persisted into the eras of anthropomorphic gods. But
the politically superior state religions which finally emerged
used their power to subdue all competitors. They drove the
earlier theriomorphic cults underground politically, and
geographically to the chthonic regions whereon they were
blackened as magic by the priestly unions. Christian
apologetics, like all political propaganda, attempted to
destroy the system in which the indigenous practitioners of
an inherited ritual found satisfaction. Voodoo offers
interesting links between state religion and so-called witchcraft.
It is the emergence of the autonomous African state which
may provide the most fruitful field for this study of collateral
descent from theriomorphic beginnings. Now that colonial
influence on native religions is less, we may see a gradual
return to indigenous cultures.

The Aurignacian Dome of Serpents at Rouffignac testifies
to the seniority of serpent worship. Residues of serpent cults

persist in myth and art-forms from Eden to Haiti. The serpent, by virtue of its sinuous movement and resting posture, its spiral tree-climbing habit and the zig-zag signs it carries on its back, was consigned to the protective, ritual role by the ancients. Because the force-field significance of its sign-form and decorative signs has not been properly understood, it has been loosely assigned to fertility cults by Europeans. In the teeming natural world, with its chemically stimulated and limited breeding seasons, reproductive exuberance is the norm and needs no cultivation. My thesis is that nature is chiefly concerned with preserving embryos from chemical sensing by distant predators.

In early man's arboreal epochs the serpent would have been a notably dangerous enemy which, when transfigured into a god, had to be placated. Omnipotent gods must be bought-off with gifts, promises and sacrifice. A cult of serpent placation, perhaps the earliest of masochistic adoration exercises, demanded a fixed liturgy which would also seek means to restrict its power by the use of its own sign. The voodoo symbol of the snake-god, Damballah-wèdo (Figure 4.1), incorporates a wealth of protective ritual detail: Plant-leaves with four shoots on the stem top; eight-limbed crosses; serpentine forms overlaid with additional herring-bone suppression; the column reinforced with lattice; and chevrons and double crosses reinforcing the centre-point of a quincunx in which the snake-god's spirit resided. During the ceremonies of the Australian Warramunga tribe the males wear the serpentine sign ⋃ painted on their chests and backs.[1] This implies a self-protective withdrawal from chemical interchange with powerful spirits on earth, perhaps from the god's deputy presumed to be present at the ceremony. Large serpentine signs on raised mounds protect the immediate area. The sign of the serpent Yarapi, painted on the surface of an overhanging rock,[2] could give magnetic sanctuary from worldly evil to an accepted initiate if he crawled into the space beneath and behind the sign.

While the bull-god may represent fertility and savage strength, the horns of his bovine deputies are not only lowered to obtain mechanical leverage for an upward blow. The bull has been an object of religious veneration in many

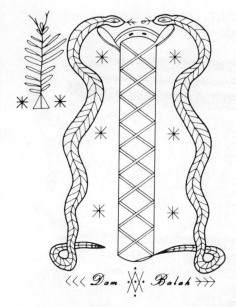

Figure 4.1   Symbol of voodoo snake-god Damballah-wèdo

ancient cults. It was used in burial ritual because of the
protective force-fields the horns provided. Often they were
mounted on poles so that overhead insulation could be
obtained. The horn sign protected the Minotaur, Hathor the
Egyptian goddess, and the Golden Calf. The bulls of Mohenjo-
Daro have horn signs on shoulders and underbelly.[3]

The Mycenaean ritual bowl (Figure 4.2) is self-suppressed
by its circular horizontal planes above and below the handles.
On its body are depicted various protective signs. On the bull's
shoulders are buckle-like suppressors, such as appeared on an
Azilian painted pebble and Spanish rock art, ⋂ . At the
waist are scale-interstice signs and on the rump eight broken
circles. The bull's eye is like the Azilian pebble's flute-and-
arris design, while meanders cover the bird's body.

The Mithraic ceremony culminated in the sacrifice of the
bull, only the finest of creatures being acceptable to the sun-
god. The horn sign is still worn by present-day native tribes
in New Guinea, by the rickshaw-boys of Durban, and North
American Indian chiefs and medicine-men. Norsemen added

its protection to their helmets. The ram's horn was used in the Hebrew religious musical instrument, the shofar.

Figure 4.2   Mycenaean ritual bowl

Horns and antlers, apart from their use as weapons, produce protective force-fields which the animal can deploy to prevent its chemical emissions from attracting distant attention. For this defence horned animals, such as the ram, rely on the spiral and curved forms in the horns, which continue to grow, while antlered creatures align and re-align the suppressive planes which operate across various four 'points' as well as employing the side curves.[4] Both sexes of the horned animals are often so equipped but in most deer species only the male is able to grow antlers, which are shed at the end of the autumn breeding season when mating contests are over. This shedding of antlers thus coincides with a time when the highly concentrated chemico-emotional state of the male may have subsided and antler weaponry and suppression is less necessary for defence. It may be a reason why most females do not need, or perhaps should not have, antler protection in our chemical context.

A bull or cow when holding its head level chemically senses the direction of potential predators through the muzzle which conducts its searching vector through the vertical force-field around its horns. When grazing in open pasture and still facing the same direction the lowered muzzle directs its searching vector to assess the chemical nutriment nearby. This posture also re-aligns the horns' shield so as to cover its muzzle's emissions against self-betrayal ahead. When confronted, a bull or cow lowers its horns in this defensive or evasive posture and the beast frequently backs away a step. A calf, when being suckled or when standing very close to its mother's side, similarly obtains chemical anonymity from a threatening quarter: the horns' front and side curves afford the same kind of chemical anonymity as a duck's deployed wing- and tail-feathers bestow on her chicks.

The corrida, which embraces the congregational liturgy of the Spanish bullfight, preserves a processional entry — the cuadrilla — of priest-like functionaries and their acolytes. A musical fanfare announces each ritual stage and the dedication of the sacrificial beast to a chosen votary precedes the death-thrust or moment of truth. The corrida is usually held on a Saint's day, which has also marked some auspicious time in the astrological calendar. The matador, perhaps alone among the lineal successors of the early sacrificial priesthood, at no time withdraws his chemical sympathy but remains *en rapport* with both the victim and his own congregation of aficionados. Priest, victim and congregation are protected from worldly contamination during the ritual within the circular and arched bullring: only the heat waves from the offered blood would ascend to the bull-god. Humans were sacrificed in this way to the anthromorphic god in early times.

It is the matador's dress which shows that he does not deny his radiant intercourse to man or beast behind any defensive thorax shield such as a cross, lunula or disc during any phase in the ritual. The signs incorporated in the front of the matador's Suit of Lights are predominantly vital, any suppressive signs being very local and in no way hindering his chemical interchange. On his shoulders are dome-suppressed, raised buttons. Other ornamental groups are in signalling triads and pentads. Even the leaf-like suppressors which appear on the suit are all contained by locally suppressive ellipses. The matador's unbuttoned bolero also bares his thoracic and solar plexus areas, the forward points of the emission of his radiance being thus open to unite with those of his adversary and of his votaries. The positioning of the horn sign on the lapel of the bolero edges is as exactly functional as is Veale's lapel-cross which prevents the Revealer operator receiving overhead signals while not impeding the emission on levels at and below the horizontal. By this lapel horn sign $\rangle$ $\langle$ the matador-priest eludes the wrath of the god for any ritual errors he may commit during preparation and dispatch of the offering. When the ritual approaches the moment of truth, the bull finally lowers his head towards the bottom of the matador's hypnotic muleta. In his exhaustion the bull interposes the magnetic-protective screen of his horns between his life-centre and his enemy in a last desperate attempt at self-insulation. In performing the estocada the matador passes through the magnetic shield to plunge home the sacrificial sword.

2 Totemism and witchcraft

A totemist religious cult aims at regaining for the tribe man's ancient anticipatory faculty for using advance chemical advice of natural changes. This is vicariously obtained through the adoption and ritual imitation of the visual behaviour of a creature which patently possesses and uses the faculty. Totemism, being derived from the ancient theriomorphic gods, suffered the patronizing attitudes of the later anthropomorphic-god schools. In retrospect, this conflict seems to stem from a simple division between the Neolithic pastoral societies and the Upper Neolithic and Bronze Age agrarians which produced the metallurgic despoiler cultures. The latter were thus one more remove from man's natural position within flora and fauna.

Émile Durkheim believed that it was not the great cosmic

powers of sun, moon, sky, mountains, sea or wind that were
first divinized as the sacred objects of nature, but the humble
vegetables and animals. He mentioned ducks, rabbits,
kangaroos, lizards, worms and frogs as typical totemic choices:
'The objective qualities surely were not the origin of the
religious sentiments which they inspired.'[5] The churinga, which
Durkheim named as the most sacred object in aboriginal
religion, is a stone or wooden oval which usually bears
protective emblems around which allegory is woven. The
signs of the churingas have been rationalized into representing
mythical situations for ritual purposes, all deriving from the
dimly remembered protective effects of the signs or sign-
forms. Durkheim continues: 'so it is this mark and this alone
which gives them their sacred character.' The churinga was
commonly supposed to carry the spirit of an ancestor. This
belief frequently accompanies miracle-making myth which
crystallizes a memory of tales concerning the early ancestor,
he who first brought the knowledge and working techniques
of the magical, protective signs to his tribe. Durkheim
remarks: 'Finally, there are whole tribes where the churinga
is never associated with a spirit.'[6]

While Durkheim believed that the emblem (only) on a
churinga constitutes its sacred character, Lévi-Strauss contests
this. He quotes T.G.H. Strehelow: 'among the Southern
Aranda he saw churinga, which are plain pieces . . . of wood
devoid of markings.'[7] Probably, Strehelow, being unaware
of the sacred, magnetic-protective property inherent in plain
objects of identical chemical material when in groups of four,
did not report in numerical detail. Graham Clark shows four
aboriginal initiates with their four sacred stones:[8] for these
potential evangelists their gospels resided in the four plain
river-smoothed pebbles held sacred in their guardianship —
sermons in stones.

Concerning their ceremonial reviews Durkheim describes as
the central object the nurtunga. This appears to be a pole with
an unsuppressed top on which altar the sacred churinga is
hung as the focal point during a ceremony. It is the totem
clan's rallying flag and seems to encapsulate the aspirations
within the race, and is similar in its cohesive effect to a
regimental colour. The nurtunga is struck or dismantled at the

end of the ceremony. The waninga, also carried to and erected on the spot, to be hauled down at the end of the ceremony, 'consists in a vertical support formed by a long stick or by a lance . . . with sometimes one and sometimes two crosspieces . . . cords . . . diagonally cross the space included between the arms of the cross . . . they form a network in the form of a lozenge.'[9] The ritual function of this cross-and-lattice suppressor is the equivalent of the processional cross, or banners with strange devices to be set up on a stand at the venue. The waninga sign-structure may proclaim the racial trust in its protection, as the Union Jack, shield and Neptune trident of Britannia — another touch derived from nature.

Durkheim should have the last, prescient word:[10]

totemism is the religion, not of such and such animal or men or images, but of an anonymous and impersonal force . . . . When we say that these principles are forces, we do not take the word in a metaphorical sense; they act just like veritable forces. In one sense, they are even material forces which mechanically engender physical effects.

The magical signs, incantations and spells employed in the rituals of witchcraft derive from the same magnetic signs of nature and the effective techniques evolved for using them by primitive man. Thus they derive from the same source as orthodox religious liturgy and ritual. The magnetic-protective force-fields surrounding cross and pentacle are the same in kind, and in effectiveness. European witchcraft practice has been reduced to minuscule proportions by emotive propaganda, and by the political and physical repression exercised through the hegemony of its better-organized, collateral relative, the king-priesthood. Through losing this power struggle witchcraft has been consigned to the nether regions inhabited by chthonic gods, while its rivals, the politically successful state-supported religions, turned their eyes towards the celestial gods. As a consequence witchcraft has become a rallying point of an underground movement of religious and social dissenters who, although motivated by the same sign-forces embedded in the unconscious mind, had their own use of them proscribed. The laws against witchcraft were repealed in Britain by the Witchcraft Act of — only — 1735.

The lack of a genuinely ancient witchcraft canon, comparable in any way with those orthodox versions derived from the sun-god and wonderfully preserved, deprives the student of valuable data which, otherwise, might have been collaterally received. It might well have helped to illuminate the Neolithic to Bronze Age hiatus in religio-social terms. Those lost millennia would surely have witnessed the sensorial descent of man from the consciously employed magnetic-protective techniques of his distant ancestors to the somnambulistic magico-symbolism of modern times.

Although society now lacks a reliable canon of witchcraft liturgy, Romanies, and other wanderers over the earth, learn some of nature's diagnoses and healing methods during their foreign encounters. Religion and healing go hand in hand. Primitive peoples had to learn to heal themselves without the benefit of a Health Service. Sophisticated societies too readily dismiss residual folk-knowledge as being rooted in superstition, quackery and so forth. The past development of homoeopathic herbal cures, deriving from the superstitious countryman who is less removed from an understanding of nature's chemical specifics and simples, has been of inestimable value to the less chemically receptive townsman. The modern pharmacopoeia, with its very successful capacity to arrest infection which the body can then overcome, has been erected on the countryman's observation and practice.

The chemical-conductance phenomenon underlies the African witch-doctor's power. His work is considered, here, by seeking to discount religious concepts of morality and orthodox scepticism. The European, in general, mis-attributes its devastating effects to psychological pressure only. The witch-doctor achieves his effects by radiational conduction. He does this secretly from a distance simply by adulterating the homing-rays which radiationally link a person with his or her dispersed bodily debris. Blood, hair, nail-parings, spittle and so on, supplied to or obtained by the witch-doctor, expose the owner to conducted absorption of energizing — or harmful — chemical matter. Although the doses so conducted are minute, the ray-bombardment is continuous by night and day, and cumulative. The witch-doctor can maintain the potency or virulence of the adulteration by replenishing the aphrodisiac or poison in which the personal debris is steeped.

It may be that Delilah weakened Samson by poisoning him by way of his shorn locks. Revealer tests suggest that the practical defence would lie in totally suppressing your house, and your person when walking about, or by recapturing and boiling the poisoned personal debris.

Purification by fire and water is manifested in the funeral pyre, burnt offerings and executions at the stake for heretical opinions. The symbolic use of incense, joss-sticks or candles, and baptism, continue the purification rituals. Hellfire and the Flood represent this in allegory.

The alchemists attempted to bridge, with an experimental chemical philosophy, the gulf which divides the ancient practical use of magnetic sign control of the chemical interchange phenomenon, and the modern, formalized sign-symbolism which is its anaemic shadow. The alchemists wavered between the magnetic characteristics of trinity and quaternity. They utilized a repeating cycle ranging from death, the separation of the constituent elements, the union of opposites — positive and negative — and back to the ever-surviving spirit: Mercurius re-emerging from the alchemical retort. Fire and water were chemical and philosophical transmuters from grossness to purity for both ancient and mediaeval priests as well as for the alchemists.

The mixture of religion and chemical experiment in alchemy was a practical exercise in a philosophy firmly based on the ever-present but unfocused memory of the complementary functions of vital chemical interchange and defensive sign-control that psychically disturbed modern man still seeks to recapture in his mandala dreams. Mysticism is the fogged memory through which philosophy peers, for ever seeking the underlying physiological secret of the *lapis*, the stone in which resides the essence of the Self, a search hitherto confined to psychoanalytical studies.

3 Ritual objects and gestures

The Horned Moon, beloved by earlier poets, epitomizes the significance of this sign to primitive man who equated the curved phases of that orb with the natural effects those stages produced on Earth. Eventually he would conclude that in certain horned phases of Luna's disc her indulgence and protection was most likely to be extended to human initiative. Man's planting rituals were thus linked with a propitious, safe time for the initiation of new life that determined a ritual calendar, the results of which still operate in the varying dates for the Christian Easter. As Hippolyta says in *A Midsummer Night's Dream*:

And then the moon, like to a silver bow
New-bent in heaven, shall behold the night
Of our solemnities.

The lunate artefact does not signal like a broken circle as its curves are eccentric: $\big)\big)$. It provides extensive suppression like an arch. Lunate ear-rings were found in the mass burials at Ur,[11] and here this protective form may have been employed to screen the wearer from the evil words and temptations heard in the profane world. The female's social use of ear-rings is to suggest a way of approach to the male. Ancient Celtic chieftains used the sign in gorgets. The lunate pectoral is still worn by natives of New Guinea at war-like ceremonials. Cart-horses wore it in brass harness ornaments to bring them luck.

Portable sign-forms, such as crossed sticks for wall suppression, led to portable sign-artefacts such as the Azilian painted pebbles. The portable Gravettian graven-images (Figure 2.2) embodied, then, the technology of physical sign-protection. These idols and dolls, Venus prototypes, were harbingers of later effigies bearing potent signs, which had protective or intercessory functions. Later, the virtue immanent in the sign itself was transferred to the named idol that displayed it. The names of the idols or representatives of the individual gods and goddesses would have been rooted in the articulated sounds given to the particular signs they carried. This suggested correlation seems impossible to trace linguistically, even for skilled philologists. When a tribal god was lost, that is when his idol was captured by another tribe, then his name was exposed to some modification of the original sign-sound. This could occur either through differences in the speech production of their captors or from their differing sign-sound values. For instance, in Semitic languages Ⅴ Ψ have the phonetic value of K, and in Greek languages Ⅴ Ⅶ have the phonetic value of P or Ps.

Anubis, who conducted the Egyptian dead to a resurrected life in the netherworld, manipulated the ritual, vitalizing, Ankh ring-sign (Figure 2.3, column 1). An or ain meant 'ring'.[12] Anu, an ancient Syrian sky-god, was displaced by Baal, whose sister-consort, the mother-goddess Anat, was in turn embodied in a composite Egyptian mother-goddess, Anta of Memphis. Hannahanna of Anatolia, Nana of Phrygia, Ninni of Elam and Ninhursag(a) of Sumeria were mother-goddesses, the modification of whose names seems to indicate a common sun-god root, An, meaning protective circle or ring. A different set of tribal phonetic values seems to explain the change in the name of the Hittite mother-goddess Hepatu to that of the Hurrian goddess Hebat or Hepit.[13] Professor James writes about 'Hannahanna, "the grandmother" whose name was written with the ideogram of the Sumerian mother goddess Nintud.'[14]

Many of the protective signs distinguishing gods and goddesses of ancient civilizations are familiar today; for example, Mercury's caduceus formed from two entwined serpents, and Poseidon's trident on its shaft. When in flight Mercury held the caduceus before him, like a modern processional cross. Aphrodite's sign, Ⴘ, placed over the pelvic area combines vulva- and cross-signs which guard that area. The protective sign of the fire-god Tjintya (cf. Q-Celtic Tienney or Tien meaning elemental fire[15]) is reminiscent of an Azilian painted-pebble sign which is identical with those buckle-type signs on the bull's shoulder on the Mycenaean bowl (Figure 4.2). One of the signs of Isis was the disc supported between the horns.

The Sumerian eye-idols of the Brak Temple, c.3211 BC (Figure 4.3), employ multiple chevrons, eight-units, ovals protecting the windows of the soul and bird and stag-horn curves, and the stag's four legs. Modern Australian Aboriginal doll-idols (Figure 4.4) personify and perpetuate ancient folk-heroes who, by enlisting the personal intervention of their god, did the tribe some great service. The wide-extent cross-signs incised into these Aboriginal dolls are obvious

Figure 4.3   Brak temple idol   Figure 4.4   Aboriginal ritual dolls

enough but, in addition, the high relief of the eyebrows and nose reproduces the horn sign and provides extra vertical planes of extensive suppression to protect the front of the chest. This last-mentioned sign appears in Kon-Tiki representations ♈ and in many other early examples of protective art.

The ritual objects of many religions show, in their phonemes and syllables, their Chen and Tien sun-god derivations: chasuble, chalice, shawm, challil, kosher, chapati, ushabtis, mutsu-shiki idols and the holy books Mishnah, Ching, Koran and Chalam Balam, etc. The kachina dolls of the Hopi Indians come into this category: they represent friendly spirits and are protected by horns, leaves, feathers and many other suppressive signs. They are impersonated in ritual dances.[16]

Effigies of the four Egyptian goddesses Neith, Isis, Serket and Nephthys were placed in protective ritual positions around the dead Pharaoh's remains. Each effigy, with its arms outspread, was in effect a suppressive cruciform. The name

103

ushabti (or shawabti), for a small tomb figurine, includes the phonemes Sha and Ti, so that their religious character is incontestable. Those sign-liveried deputies of the gods bore many suppressive hieroglyphs on their dress, which afforded further magnetic protection for the dead Pharaoh. When crossed hoes were carried in their representations this may have signified the protection of agriculture. However, their crossed hoes, crossed arms, or wing-feathers crossed over their breasts, added practical protection to the royal corpse. Arranged in the tomb near to the separately incarcerated visceral remains the ushabtis' role was one of supplementing or deputizing for those Egyptian gods and goddesses that were prominently identified in the burial rites. Much later, when rationalized by priestly policy-makers, the ushabtis seem to have been relegated to the discharge of menial chores for the dead in the after-life. From the evidence of the magnetic protection afforded both by their forms and sign-embellishments this seems to have been an unwarranted demotion of function.

Figure 4.5   Statue of the 'Ka' of the King Hor. Dahshur, late XIIth Dynasty

Egyptologists are doubtful as to the real significance of the ritual Ka gesture (Figure 4.5). We have encountered this protective phoneme and its suppressive script signs before (Figure 2.4). This gesture has been described as a manifestation of vital energy, as the creator and sustainer of life. It is said to be particularly relevant when referring to the dead.[17] However, the overhead suppressive force-field around the upraised fingers, which form four-multiple layers down to the thumbs, is suggested by the low placing of the thumbs. The effect of this gesture is to escape the attention of the Cosmic Force, rather than receive vital energy from above.

A human subject, when tested for the Ka effect, was placed in a lounge immediately beneath a bedroom which represented the heavens. First, his personal radiations were found to be reaching the Revealer operator placed above. On receiving a stamping signal from overhead the subject raised his hands in the Ka position. The signals then failed to reach the operator upstairs showing that the subject's radiations had been interrupted by the sign. Whether the protective force-fields so produced form separately around each four-finger group, which then overlaps that of the other hand, or whether one larger area of suppression forms around the eight fingers, would seem to depend on the lateral separation of the hands. The experiment with the Ka overhead protection was repeated downstairs with the subject sitting on the carpet. With the instrument projected over his head and hands, the suppression continued.

Variations in the use of eight fingers, which produce defensive force-fields continuing in layers and ending at the thumbs, can be found in several familiar ritual gestures. For instance, the hands placed palms together, with the eight fingers projected straight ahead and at breast-level, insulates the user from worldly contamination or chemically emotive distractions from in front. The forward-facing eight knuckles of clasped hands, with either the thumbs tucked in behind them or upraised and crossed in the vertical plane, form the Roman Catholic prayer gesture, which also insulates the supplicant from frontal, chemical interchange. A recumbent effigy — for example, a knight's tomb of former times — with its palms together and with its stone fingers pointing upwards, suggests overhead magnetic protection of the body below. In the flesh, this gesture produces a protective effect similar to that of a Pharaoh's recumbent body-effigy with arms crossed across the chest.

The rejection gesture, which literally and figuratively pushes away the threat of an apprehended danger, is made with the palms of the hands presented outwards in front of the body with the extended fingers slightly in advance. This produces a near-vertical force-field across and down the eight fingers and effectively stops the subject from chemically corresponding with the danger ahead. The common greeting gesture for 'welcoming with open arms' allows the projection of vital and sympathetic radiance. This is because the welcomer's body, with legs apart, adopts the form of a five-pointed star. The arms are flung wide apart with the planes of the fingers obliquely outwards and away from the body's emission point. However, when the naked ankles touch each other that posture of the body forms a cruciform and no radiance is emitted forwards. These differing postures have all been tested on the human subject.

The position of the feet of Jesus on the cross has been much debated: both alternatives cited below would have produced frontal magnetic protection of His body. With the feet not touching each other, and four nails being employed, the tetramorph of nails forms the suppression. If one foot were placed on the other and only three nails were used the body itself would form a cruciform of protection. The wooden cross would similarly protect His back and the halo signify the local, overhead protection of a circle.

Regal and priestly processions behind an upheld suppressive device, be it cross, crook, olive-branch, palm-branch or feathered fan, are magnetically debarred from chemical communication with the good as well as being shielded from the evil emanations of the profane world which they are approaching. The ceremonial progress of the wife of a chief of the Timucuas of Florida, as depicted by de Bry, shows the arrangement from which we can deduce that the leafy bower, constructed on the litter, provides rear, side, and overhead magnetic protection for the occupant. Attendants carrying upheld fans give frontal protection to the chief's wife, while feathers in their hair assist suppression at lower levels.[18]

The ritual exclusiveness and withdrawal from the secular world of the king and high priest has always been used to impress the laity. A Chinese Buddha may be shown wearing a swastika on his chest with meander-sign embroidery on his clothes; Tiglath-Pileser III of Assyria has been depicted with a large pectoral Maltese cross. A bishop unwittingly reduces his impact on his flock as he withdraws his radiant personality from the congregation of believers and doubting Thomases. This is because he is sheltering behind the magnetic protection of his pectoral cross. The cross, by its size, rigidity and location, physically blocks the emergence of his chemical radiance, which otherwise could faintly resonate sympathetic chords of chemically stimulated emotion in a latently responsive following. If the priest finds himself more and more neglected through this retreat from chemical communion with his flock, it would at least help to restore the physical, sympathetic bond with them if he were to shift his pectoral cross to his side during an address to the congregation.

Gregarious mankind needs the living communion of such radiant intercourse, a sharing of an original endowment within his own species. From this he can draw comfort and nurture generosity simply through benevolent human propinquity which facilitates interchange on shared wave lengths. In the secular sphere more and more young people wear suppressive signs on their chests, while only rarely does one see a vital sign such as the Ankh being worn. It would be unwise to read too much into this trend towards ornaments which physically contain the projective power of human radiation. That it might reflect youth's deeply felt withdrawal from stereotyped institutions and party politics seems just possible. While there is an unconscious recourse to archetypal protective signs in times of great anxiety and frustration — as has been shown by Jung — there remains the possibility that in youth this perception may be subliminal rather than unconscious, as mostly occurs in middle-aged and elderly people. I am aware that even a demure little cross when worn as a pendant inevitably leads the male eye to a girl's bosom, but this, like the underlying suggestion of ear-rings, is a social use of ornament.

Humanism inclines to the idea that ethical development depends mostly on individual cultivation. But herd compulsions in our gregarious species are much more ancient and deep-seated than modern intellectual philosophies, so individual effort cannot hope to supplant the communal reassurance and strength gained from even a temporarily united concourse, especially under the stimulus of a benignly radiating pastor. The one universal link between all races on earth is manifest in sign-ritual common to all religious liturgies. All are colts bred from the self-same Aurignacian and Palaeolithic stables: only the trainers and riders have changed. Jung calls the tetramorph, 'the steed of the Church'.[19]

Multiples of the tetramorph are the very substance of religious history. The four-limbed cross is the protector of the Son. There are four gospels, evangelists, winds, sons of Horus, seasons, cardinal points, elements (fire, water, sky and earth). The eight-limbed cross is the protector of the Father. There were eight in Noah's family — Noah, his wife, Ham, Shem, Japheth and their three wives. The octamorph is the Muhammadan sign manifest in carpet design, architecture and the eight gates of Paradise. It is a mandala sub-division. There are twelve apostles, tribes of Israel, signs of the Zodiac (with their protective signs), months of the year, items in a dozen, people in a jury, former pence in a shilling. There are sixteen petals in the Japanese royal emblem, the chrysanthemum. A folk song, 'Queen Mary, Queen Mary, my age is sixteen', suggests legal protection through the age of consent. There are twenty-four hours of the day, and there were twenty-four elders in Ezekiel's vision. There are thirty-two mysterious paths of wisdom in the Sepher Yetsirah, and thirty-two Mahavyanja fortunate signs of the Buddha child.[20]

The concept of spiritual regeneration through vigil, ordeal and self-discipline is woven around the numerical referent forty: days in Lent; days of quarantine;[21] days of the Flood; years in the wilderness; days and nights of Moses on the Mount; years of Philistine domination of Israel; days of purification after childbirth; Jonah's warning to Nineveh; and many others.

Childhood nightmares, so vivid with their threatening pictures of animals, are terrifying. Jung has shown, so convincingly, that the psyche stores packages of mandalas to protect us against the ancient beasts in their dream forms — demons, dragons or our own mental situations. A dream, reported by Jung, was described thus: 'An actor smashes his hat against the wall where it looks like this' (Figure 4.6).

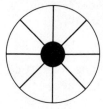

Figure 4.6   Hat as a protective mandala

Surely this suggests one original function of the hat as a mandala. The circular tonsure, the dome-like clerical cap, the crown-circlet, mitre, biretta, laurel wreath and the nimbus (head-halo) give sign-form protection as well as providing head-covering. When a stage in the ritual was reached which required the priest, personally, to supplicate his god, the suppressive headgear was removed and he moved away from beneath the suppressive roof sections. He then stood before the altar, which in ancient times was in the open air, under the uninhibited scrutiny of his god. The priest tilting back his head and gazing skyward symbolically alters the plane of suppression of his tonsured head-circle and offers himself openly to the radiance from above.

The anointing of a king requires the absence of the vertically protective crown so that he may partake of a heavenly authority. The horizontal planes of suppression afforded by the simple circlet did not give complete overhead insulation. The circlet was extended both vertically and laterally in the later crown. This was done by placing crosslets, or fleurs-de-lis of tetra- or octamorphic form, around and projecting above the circlet's band in groups of four, eight, and so on. The vertical planes of each individual crosslet and fleur-de-lis give extensive and overlapping shielding against lateral contamination. The horizontal planes across the four-multiple tops of the crosslets and fleurs-de-lis are repeated down the uprights, thus extending the vertical protection well above and below the circlet's original limits. The Roman emperor's bay-laurel or oak-leaf wreath similarly afforded shields of suppressive leaves which, in the making and wearing of the wreath, become aligned along many different vertical and oblique planes. This gave all-round defensive screening down to at least chest level. Garlands are worn around the neck when protection of the whole chest is desired.

The front and rear arch shapes of the mitre often carry additional suppressive signs such as a pair of spirals or a lattice design: this headgear gives lateral, oblique and overhead protection. The North American Indian chief and medicine-man carry a sceptre of a single feather, a feather bunch, or a lance with feathers attached down its shaft, which is held in front of the body as protection from baneful radiation. The British colonial governor-general and the field-marshal perpetuate this feather protection in their ceremonial head-dress. Parasols and umbrellas of state give local, overhead suppression; a quincunx of finials on the roof of a state coach provides a radiational pyramid to protect the occupants.

A tested cowrie shell of the species *Cypraea tigris* L., 7·5 cm long and 5·5 cm across its widest section, gave a suppressive radius of 29 cm beyond its visible limits of length, breadth and depth. The cowrie is used in protective masks and necklaces because of the extensive force-field produced by the meander sign across the bottom of the shell. This sign is worn outwards.[22] The cowrie was used for coinage and its talismanic protection is continued in metal coins which carry suppressive signs on one side or the other, or both. The coin's purpose, apart from a means of barter, was to protect the king's image, or at least its back. By inference the king conferred this protection on the temporary owner of the coin. Familiar coin suppressive signs are the cross, leaves, birds, and Britannia's trident and cross-signed oval shield. This system of kingly protection derived from a time when crude pieces of metal did service for coins. Modern circular coins with raised rims seem to curtail the wide-extent effectiveness of the protective signs on them.

4 An original function of dance

The domesticated dog, when it circles before lying down for
a rest, is obeying an archetypal compulsion. It is treading down
a mat, and making an enclosing 'basket' of vegetation stalks
of the same chemicals. This action will form lattice-work to
magnetically protect this sanctuary against distant detection.
In modern times the circular perambulation of a site —
originally to imprint in the ground an enclosing circle — marks
the commencement of a Roman Catholic religious foundation.
Ritual 'dances' in birds and other creatures have attracted
human attention but mostly concerning courtship and
aggression.

The dances of humans, received by way of folk-memory and
tradition, are often rationalized as fanciful allegory, sometimes
with a moral aspect. But surviving folk-dances, if they have
the right number of participants and follow their original
intention, employ two phases. The first one is the protective
dance plan itself. The object of this is to purify the ground
by insulating it: from above by the woven sign-patterns;
laterally, by joining hands; and below ground through the
foot-patterns trodden into the surface. The second phase is
the simple abandonment of the protective postures. This
opens the site to overhead and lateral radiation and the
dancers then mingle freely.

Tree- and plant-worship, together with natural sign-
adaptations, survive in many ritual dances. Some have been
beautifully presented in recent times by Litz Pisk,[23] one of
which is illustrated in the ground plan of the Paesont-Braule
(Figure 4.7). In this plan the external six points mark the
limits of the radiational encroachments of the outside world.
The protection of the precinct commences with the spirals
and crossings outside the circle. Within the circle the
serpentines and crossings reinforce the protection of the vital
centre in this terpsichorean mandala. The purified site will
be open after the dance has ensured its suitability for a great
enterprise or occasion.

Joan Lawson alludes to the associations of ancient tree-
worship and describes some relevant behaviour of primitive
man: 'He broke branches from the tree and swept them over

the ground in an ever widening circle . . . he linked his branch with the next man ensuring that the enclosed space would remain clear of evil until the ritual was over.'[24] A woodcut by de Bry, showing a fertility cleansing rite affords an opportunity for detailed analysis of the techniques employed (see Figure 4.8).

Figure 4.7   Ground plan of the Paesont-Braule

This ritual fertility dance of the American Indians of Virginia shows a three-circle precinct. Within the inner circle, and upon the centre, stand three (that is, vital-numbered) virgins. Circles cut in the turf block the chemical emissions from the evil chthontic gods below ground. For lateral protection the three virgins cross their arms over each other's backs and bend their legs knees-to-knees, presenting three facets of opposed chevron pairs. They are open to heavenly radiance which travels down their vital triskelion-form heads and trunks. The vital-numbered seven phallic poles indicate the upward signalling capability of the enclosed precinct. The circular corridor between the outermost circle and the pole-circle protects the officiants standing there from below ground. With their leafy branch suppressors they give lateral protection from the intrusion of mundane spirits.

The Zulus employed a similar system. They manned two concentric circles around the central area wherein the important conclaves were held. Each man held a leafy branch so that the leaves' force-fields merged in complete lateral protection around each circle.

Figure 4.8   Ritual fertility dance of the American Indians of Virginia

A good example of an ancient ritual being preserved by folklore is found in the celebrations of Helston's Flora Day on 8 May.[25] The early morning Hal-an-Tow ceremony is derived from protective tree-ritual. Its application, here, is the cutting of magnetic-protective leafy boughs — usually of the early sycamore — which trophies are borne home by the people with ritual music, so that the protection of the newly opened leaves might be conferred on their dwellings. A primitive hunting ploy preventing the hunter's chemical detection by the quarry is symbolized here: compare Birnam Wood coming to Dunsinane in *Macbeth*. The St Michael and Dragon myth, as enacted during the Helston Flora celebrations, seems to be a very recent Christian scion grafted on to the ancient Hal-an-Tow trunk. St Michael, under the protection of his mock plumed helmet, defeats the latent threat of the ancient predatory beasts of cave-dwelling times now syncretistically symbolized as a cardboard dragon.

As already described, the suppressive framework of a North American Indian tepee required one less than a four-multiple of poles in the peristyle,   if a   central one completed the magnetic protection. The same ground protection is achieved if the number of people holding ribbons attached to a Maypole is one less than a four-multiple; the be-ribboned pole then completes the four-multiple of ribbon units.

Many games derive from ritual protective origins, for instance 'hopscotch' which is played on ground suppressed with a lattice. The game 'noughts and crosses' completely reflects the sanctuary influence. A pack of cards contains four suits and fifty-two cards. At Ur, in the Chaldees, a gaming-board was used in which the 'squares' were embellished with the protective quincunx, octamorphs guarding a holy centre, tetramorphs and lattice. Each player had (vital-numbered) seven 'men', or counters, which bore the quincunx sign.[26]

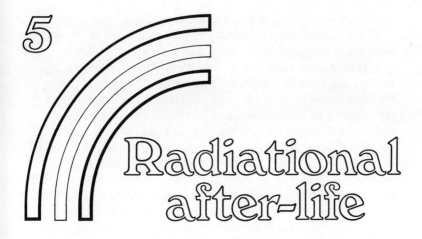

5 Radiational after-life

1 The essence-bone

The belief in an after-life has endured for millenia. In the radiational sense this seems to be well founded. I made some Revealer tests over lightly calcined bones contained in an oblong Iron Age kist-vaen which had been excavated at Pelynt in Cornwall. An approximate date of 1000 BC had been assigned to the remains. The first test showed that the unique personal signals from separately removed bones were still resonating with others of the same person in the stone coffin. This indicated that the personality of the individual was persisting in its broadcast after a time lapse of some 3,000 years. The next test was for the persistence of some of the soluble chemicals, normal to the mammalian complement, which would have been absorbed into the bones during life. This test indicated that eleven out of the twelve tested items were still signalling. Only one item, potassium chloride, did not respond.

An opportunity offered itself for the testing of a Pliosaur's fossilized vertebral bone, which was still signalling both the personal and general chemical content. Nine out of the test series of twelve were signalling normally. The age of the specimen was put at something around 150 million years.

The personal essence which survives death can be shown to issue from one particular bone in a vertebrate's skeleton. This also appears to be the radiational base where the searching vectors for homing and food location originate. This one vertebra interchanges with all dispersed debris items from the owner's body and over any terrestial distance unless suppressors intervene. During further tests for persistence of the signal of what I call the essence-bone, I visited the burial places of several members of my own family. Matching samples, such as hair and photographs, disclosed the ray-paths leading up to the grave and culminated with the instrument crossing-over in a position over the essence-bone. None of these graves was suppressed by signs.

The first experiment to isolate the essence-bone in a skeleton was made with the vertebrae of a plaice. The plaice was first broken into two approximate halves which were placed in separate parts of the house and garden, avoiding any chance suppression by leaves. The retained matcher, a fin from the fish's body, enabled the personally-signalling half to be directionally detected. This signalling section was progressively reduced and the dispersal of those remnants continued until only the essence vertebra still signalled. In the many plaice, soles and flounders tested, the essence-bone was found to be always in precisely the same position in the skeleton of each individual. This bone is classified as the fourth caudal vertebra (see Figure 5.1 (a)).

Tests were made on a human male skeleton in a museum. It was found that the pendulous tip of the fourth thoracic vertebra was the actual point of contact which restored the signals during a 'suppress and recover' test drill. A ring was attached to the skeleton over the essence-bone to mark its position in a photograph. Two other tests were made, this time on the back of two living persons. The relative positions of the essence-bone in humans and plaice suggest joint ancestry (see Figure 5.1 (b)).

Primitive man, still sensitive to chemical radiation, would be well aware of the persistence of a parent's personal body-signals after death, as they would have the same vibratory characteristics, or 'note', which had distinguished them in

life. If the signals were such as would be perceived when
holding a relic bone, then death was only a change of state
and appearance. The relic of a saint interchanged with his
essence-bone in death; that is, until both were protected from
mundane contamination within a suppressed reliquary or
shrine.

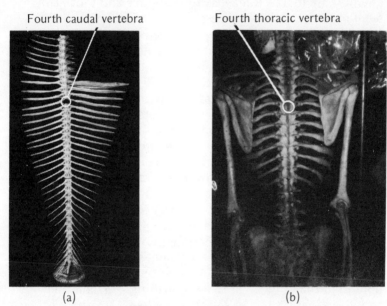

Figure 5.1 The essence-bone in plaice and human

Skull and mandible preservation cults far antedate
Palaeolithic times, reaching back to pre-Chelle-Acheulian,
Olduvian or Tanganyika man, as cited by Dr Margaret Murray.
Later, Acheulian man also preserved the head, mandible
bones and teeth, as were found at Choukoutien, China.[1]
There was perhaps a contemporary awareness that food-
advertising chemical signals issuing from these bone collections
would link them to human and animal predators. So they
were magnetically protected by sign-form arrangements such
as circles of earth or stone, or suppressive constructions of
animal horns, and so on.

117

The essence-bones seem to have been missing from all of those reported caches. Only remnants from the top of the spine would be attached to a beheaded skull. We may guess that the essence-bone usually remained at the place of death. It might have been thought that its removal would cause the spirit's loss of location and that a similar retribution would attend those who violated such an important religious sanction. Be that as it may, skull, mandible and tooth cults seem much more likely to be the result of trophy-hunting than of ancestor worship and, in consequence, magnetic protection in those cases insured the collection against their location by other plunderers, human or animal.

In Western religions the idea that soul and body are separate items in man is comparatively modern, and seems to stem from Greek philosophy. Other tests with the Revealer, using a child's photograph and his hair sample, showed them to be resonating with the mother's photograph taken during her pregnancy with that child. So we come to the conclusion that the unique, personal signal of an individual is established before birth and can continue during and after life for millions of years in suitable circumstances.

The writings of ancient and modern philosophers, who have had an intuitive way of interpreting the manifestations of the chemical communication phenomenon, seem to confirm these findings. J.E. Cirlot writes about St Augustine that 'he alludes to the value of all things in nature — organic and inorganic — as bearers of spiritual messages by virtue of their distinctive forms and characteristics',[2] and of Boethius that he, too, 'had alluded earlier to a "common rhythm" when he asserted that only things which have the same matter in common — meaning in the context, the same vital aspect — can naturally transform and interchange themselves'.[3] Jung writes:[4]

> Not only is the self indefinite but — paradoxically enough — it also includes the quality of definiteness and even of uniqueness . . . . The inclusion in a religion of a unique human personality — especially when conjoined to an indeterminable divine nature — is consistent with the absolute individuality of the self, which combines uniqueness with eternity and the individual with the universal.

The security of the self, mankind's innermost reality, and the uniqueness of the soul, is the constant care of every creature that acknowledges, with its bare existence, the creative and re-creative energizing and transmuting force of God-in-Nature. The essence-bone is thus the centre of personal radiant energy, the hub around which the life and actions of all vertebral creation revolves. It is often symbolized as a centre-point or triskelion within a circle's magnetic protection. Man thus identifies himself with the triskelion representing Cosmic Source (Father), Regeneration (Son), and Enduring God-essence (Holy Spirit). The Father is represented by the eight-limbed cross, the Son by the four-limbed cross and the Holy Spirit by the six-limbed vital cross: a Norman tympanum at Rame church in Cornwall illustrates this.[5]

A total of seven vital six-point stars are inspiring the philosopher who is unsuppressed overhead and thus ready to receive beneficent animation from above (Figure 5.2). The

Figure 5.2   Inspiration and protection of the philosopher

meditator crosses his arms for frontal protection, and the cherubim, with outstretched wings, guard his sides, thus completing his insulation from worldly intrusions of any kind.

The Egyptian god sign for 'Re' or 'Ra', and many triskelion designs found in magatamas, are enclosed within circles and thus symbolize protection or containment of the central, spiritual essence. The Devil — man's alter ego — could be impounded and neutralized within a circle of priestly vigilance (see Figure 5.3).

Donald McKenzie, illustrating a Japanese triskelion example, describes magatamas as curved jewels, comma-like symbols.[6] Our interest, here, is with the numerical protection of four-multiple repetitions within the overall magnetic protection of the circles guarding the Holy Centre. McKenzie points out that there are 40 small discs, each one enclosing 3 comma-like magatamas in triskelion form, and that there are 16 more discs on the outer rim. He equates the 120 magatama commas on the 40 discs with the 120 degrees of the Babylonian Zodiac.

Figure 5.3　The Devil magnetically constrained

There were 120 'sars', or divine years, which became the basis for calculating the time-span of the four Hindu Mythical Ages, the first of which numbered 4,800 years, a total identical with the first of four pre-Columbian time-spans calculated by the Mexicans.[7] Here is a plethora of four-multiples indeed; in addition to the four-multiple discs in the circular enclosure there are 48 obelisk-type signs in this Japanese example. McKenzie continues: 'The magatama beads were placed in graves, offered to ancestral spirits and worn by the living. They were not merely "fertility" symbols, in the narrow sense of the term, but symbols representing highly complex beliefs connected with the idea of cosmic energy.'[8] Indeed their practical as well as symbolic function was to protect the centre of man's energy source and soul, the self in the essence-bone.

Artistry in the construction and elaboration of religious ornament in jewel, textile, woodwork, metal, stone and plaster, is to be found everywhere. The fact that function takes pride of place in nature's constructions makes it possible that human conceptions of beauty are determined by an archaic response to the force-fields of signs and sign-structures. The harmonies of strength, stability and proportion, evolved through a successful technology for the survival of so many species of shell-molluscs, have tutored mankind. But the pristine use of sign-structured architecture and artefacts in temples and shrines was to achieve both radiational vitality and protection without which the very reason for those edifices disappears. Beauty was not only in the eye of the beholder but also served his radiational inheritance.

The security of the immortal self within the essence-bone after death is the prime concern of all royal funeral furnishing and burial arrangements. This is evident in the succession of coffins which held Tutankhamen's skeletal remains. The central device for protecting the thorax area from above was his crossed arms with the extension of crossed crook and flail. This protection was repeated on the top surface of each of the three coffins, and in the small sarcophagi which contained his visceral remains. There are many other subsidiary protective devices, such as the sign-marked beard, the *appliqué* eyebrow

121

arches, and the four-sector chords in the top section of the nemset head-dress formed by the glass-paste bands raised on the gold plating.[9]

The funeral suit of the Chinese Princess Tou Wan shows all of the cross suppressors concentrated on the upper part of the body. The essential area of thorax suppression, giving protection to the essence-bone, is covered in all directions. Four leopard figurines gave tetramorphic protection within the princess's tomb; each bore spots in cruciform with a dot in each centre.[10]

Figure 5.4 Princess Tou Wan's funeral suit

2 The consequences of chemical alienation

The loss of the primordial chemical interchange faculty, with which protoplasm had been singularly endowed for absorbing like-chemicals from its environment, has led man to expel himself from the Eden of the full sensorial state, which expulsion has left a deep, psychic scar. Man's sensorial self-emasculation is rendered in the myth of Attis who castrated himself beneath a pine tree which shielded his act from the

Figure 5.5   Protection by cross, quincunx, four-multiples, wing-feathers, etc.

gods. Man's inner despair and tension stems from chronic remorse for the loss, by neglect, of a birthright. Psychopathic degrees of this condition result in an enlarged and inflamed ego intended to supersede the better self. Urbanized man, withdrawn from the nomad's resonating harmonies within nature's universal chemical communication system, attempts, in his dissonant psychic distress, to compensate for the sensorial loss by developing an elaborate, conscious intelligence. His most lasting compensatory achievement is religion. Through religion man expresses a well-founded faith in the natural protection and the potent radiance inherent in the cosmos.

Temporary relief from mankind's despair and tension caused by sensorial devastation is unconsciously obtained through the catharsis of dreams. The clinical studies by Jung of mandalas show how these manifestations of archetypal signs can help. Jung's patient, his psyche desperately disorientated, invokes in dream the defensive power of circle, cross and tetraktys, often in elaborate mandala forms (see Figure 5.5). Jung chose the term 'mandala' for these patterns of his dream analyses since the word denotes the ritual or magic circle.[11] The origin of the mandala form, so deeply embedded in the collective unconscious, lay in the circular rings in the horizontal stem sections of a plant or tree. Figure 5.6 shows a plant root's centre with its mandala protection as magnified under the microscope: the primary xylem is the self. O. La Farge describes a Navajo sand-painting as follows: 'In the center is a sacred, never-failing lake, from which grow corn of four colours, squash, beans, and other plants. Four rainbow bars surround the lake, on which stand gods who are invited to be present at the ceremony carrying a variety of sacred objects . . . .'[12] The vital lake is the Holy Centre within this elaborate mandala. The person who has studied my previous analyses of signs will easily recognize the ingredients in the many protective signs within the rainbow arch.

What path will modern man follow in the future if, indeed, he has any enduring future here on earth? Insensitive to chemically broadcast advice, and to warnings of razed and polluted natural environments, he industrializes his way to eventual oblivion. He continues to destroy his own living conditions and those of myriads of organisms which support flora in her purposefully controlled evolution. Man, like all fauna, is utterly dependent on flora. The foundation of man's road to self-destruction is not difficult to excavate. It was laid down during his expulsion from Eden, an allegory of his former complete sensorial communion with God-in-Nature whereby all creation prospered until intellectual knowledge became the sin which supplanted his primary sense of chemical resonance.

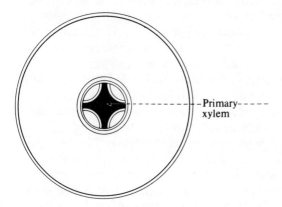

Figure 5.6   Plant-root mandala

Wild creatures are stimulated for breeding by flora's awakening broadcasts. In man's primitive and nomadic state, population movements were controlled by the natural ecological resources of each locality. Farming, by artificially increasing the availability of local foods, encouraged off-season breeding, thus altering the natural balance. When the enlarged populations experienced drought, storm, tempest and crop failure, warfare followed. Tribal extermination was necessary for local survival when the promise of increased food by artificial means collapsed.

Zoologists and other scientists have, hitherto, been forced to rationalize plant and animal behaviour within mankind's own depleted sensorial limits. Lorenz once commented on the visible deterioration in an ape community's behaviour when caged. Most cages of present design are effective suppressors of the chemical interchange effect. Consequently most caged birds and other animals, with no signal-receptive rooms or areas, are denied nature's daily and seasonal chemical bulletins and thus lack necessary stimuli or depressants during seasonal changes. Perhaps this man-made chemical isolation of caged creatures is merciful under such imprisoned circumstances. Their situation is comparable with that of a human prisoner, in long, solitary confinement, if he were to be denied every single item of news, or other contacts with the outside world, which might upset him if he were continually reminded of what he was missing.

The rape of flora is conducted on two fronts. On one side man presumes to interfere with natural processes by 'improving' plants, guided only by his own subjective intellectual fancies concerning shape, colour, scent, yield and so on. During this interference man jeopardizes their inherent qualities of hardiness, natural chemical balance and resistance to disease, and adaptability to a worsening environment of which he, himself, is the debaser. Some botanical technicians have worked to produce a leafless pea plant.[13] Being unaware of the magnetic protective function of leaves, both in relation to their own plant and to the creatures which also use that protection, they have confused cleverness with wisdom. Man, by de-horning his domestic cattle, deprives them of a part of their magnetic protective inheritance.

Man's other direction of attack on flora and her dependants derives from a relish for unsensed alterations in the natural scene. This is manifest in defoliation programmes by the military, and by developers who continue to cut great swathes into the remaining virgin forests in order to 'open up' land for industrial development. In the process the habitats of countless creatures, whose functions are essential to life-sustaining flora, are obliterated. To this is added the chain reaction of death to flora's insect, fish, bird and animal employees, set in motion by chemical spraying, polluting industrial effluent and oil, and, in the future, the danger of chemical pollution from radiating, irreducible nuclear waste.

The appalling risks inherent in any nuclear programme cannot be discounted by fallible human precautions.

Revealer experiments show that chemicals, when oscillated by cosmic radiation, are linked in resonant interchange with their exactly co-oscillating chemical counterparts over considerable distances on the earth's surface. To interrupt this resonant correspondence nuclear waste must be buried beyond the depth of cosmic-ray penetration. However, there will always be a 'time-lag' before such very deep burials can be done; so, much nuclear waste,will always be co-resonating on the ground surface on the Revealer frequencies which cannot be detected by a Geiger counter. If, as seems possible, the radioactive factors in the nuclear chemical waste are also co-resonating on this chemical interchange frequency, then a continuous, unperceived interchange of poisonous energy could offer an insidious but terrible threat to flora and fauna in the long term. In such a situation a very slow but steady process of cellular mutation and destruction will cause the eventual extinction of most present forms of life on earth. In contrast with such creeping degeneration the inevitable but relatively localized holocausts, which are bound to occur sooner or later through human error or intention, will be less terrifying: they will be plainly recognized for what they are.

Primary cosmic rays are filtered by the atmosphere which, at present, still allows the passage of the secondary cosmic radiation which sustains living cells through oscillation. Poisonous chemicals from industrial effluent and nuclear explosion can become suspended in rain clouds. So the preservation of the atmosphere's *status quo* is crucial to all present life-forms. As Georges Lakhovsky reported, pigeons were disorientated when released too near to a broadcasting radio station. This was almost certainly due to a radio frequency's harmonic overriding the natural homing frequency. Man's tendency to employ still higher radio frequencies for space travel, and so on, may eventually cause some local 'jamming' of nature's fundamental wavelengths of chemical advice and thus deprive flora of her grounded insect collaborators in many specialized environments.

Ishmael, post-nomadic man, with his departure from chemical sympathy with other living creatures and plants, is unique among sentient creation. Consequently this chemical insensitivity must be related to his shortsighted and lethal chemical expedients to satisfy the industrial Moloch. The twentieth century could, with justification, be labelled by mid-future survivors as the era of ignorant, blanket chemical pollution. The only hope for all genera and species rests on modern man rapidly recapturing a clear understanding of nature's primary sense and its cosmic-radiation support. Then, perhaps even at this late polluted hour, flora and her dependants may survive for a little longer than now seems likely in these times of plutonium fascination. It is imperative that twentieth-century urbanized man adopts a path to wisdom and gives absolute priority to the study and harnessing of the purer energy which is still showered continuously on the earth by the Cosmic God. The sickening alternative is a merely clever but temporary Faustian compact with Pluto, for which a deteriorating posterity will have to pay the twentieth century's price.

Notes

Introduction

1   Sir William Barrett and Theodore Besterman, *The Divining-Rod*, Methuen, London, 1926, p.xxii.
2   *Ibid.*, p.16.
3   *Ibid.*, p.7.
4   *Nature*, vol. 253, 17 January 1975, p.147.
5   *Op. cit.*, pp.270-6; M. Faraday, 'Experimental investigation of table turning', *Athenaeum*, July 1853, pp.801-3.
6   S.W. Tromp, *Psychical Physics*, Elsevier, New York and Amsterdam, 1949, p.307.
7   L. Watson, *Supernature*, Hodder & Stoughton, London, 1973, p.117.
8   H.S. Burr and F.S.C. Northrop, 'The Electro-dynamic theory of life', *Quarterly Review of Biology*, vol. X, No.3, September 1935, p.325.

Chapter 1 Primary perception in living creatures

1   George de la Warr, 'In retrospect', *Mind and Matter*, vol.II, no.2, September 1958, pp.13-15.
2   Louis Vaczek, *The Enjoyment of Chemistry*, Allen & Unwin, London, 1965, p.125.
3   *Ibid.*, p.141.
4   Edward O. Wilson, 'Pheromones', *Scientific American*, May 1963, p.100.

5   Sold by New Era Laboratories, London EC1.
6   Georges Lakhovsky, *The Secret of Life: Cosmic Rays and Radiations of Living Beings*, trans. M. Clement, Heinemann, London, 1939, p.32.
7   Duff Hart-Davis, *The Zodiac*, magazine of Cable & Wireless Ltd, London, May 1969, p.2.
8   *Op. cit.*, pp.32-3.
9   Roy Bedichek, *The Sense of Smell*, Michael Joseph, London, 1960, p.88.
10   *Ibid.*, p.97.
11   Observations made in Nanjizal Bay, St Levan, Cornwall, August 1966 and 1967.
12   Rutherford Platt, *The Living World*, Souvenir Press, London, 1964, pp.160,161.
13   *Ibid.*, p.165.
14   C.B. Williams, *Insect Migration*, Collins, London, 1958, p.112.
15   *Ibid.*, p.115.
16   *Ibid.*, p.41.
17   'Prospecting by photography', in de la Warr, *op. cit.*, pp.47-52.
18   G. Beiser and A. Beiser, *The Story of Cosmic Rays*, Dent, London, 1964, p.44.
19   H. Weaver, 'Locating persons missing at sea, using V-rays', *Coastguard*, Vol.2 (New series), no.1, January 1968, pp.4-5.
20   Eric Maple, *Magic, Medicine and Quackery*, Hale, London, 1968, p.96.

Chapter 2 Physical properties of signs

1   Ramona Morris and Desmond Morris, *Men and Snakes*, Hutchinson, London, 1965, p.10.
2   L.P. Garcia *et al.*, *Prehistoric and Primitive Art*, Thames & Hudson, London 1967, p.87, fig.124.
3   A. Laming, *Lascaux*, Penguin Books, Harmondsworth, 1959, pp.157-8.
4   Hans Jensen, *Sign, Symbol and Script*, Allen & Unwin, London, 1970, p.37.
5   Juan Kelly, *The Manx Dictionary*, Douglas, Isle of Man, 1846.
6   Alfred Kallir, *Sign and Design*, Clarke, Cambridge, 1960, p.131.
7   Judges 12: 5,6.
8   W. Keble Martin, *The Concise British Flora in Colour*, Ebury Press and Michael Joseph, George Rainbird, 1965, plates 71,84.
9   Paul Jaeger, *The Wonderful Life of Flowers*, Harrap, London, 1960, p.110.

10 W.W. Robbins, T.E. Weier and C.R. Stocking, *Botany: An Introduction to Plant Science*, Wiley, New York, London and Sydney (international ed.), 1966, p.35, fig. 4.11.
11 *Ibid.*, p.86, fig.7.14B.
12 Roland Green, *How I Draw Birds*, A. & C. Black, London, 1951, p.13.
13 *Ibid.*, p.82.
14 *Ibid.*, p.83.
15 W.S. Bristowe, *The World of Spiders*, Collins, London, 1970, p.121, fig.56.
16 *Ibid.*, plate XXXI.
17 *Ibid.*, p.141, fig.71.
18 F.D. Ommanney *et al.*, *The Fishes*, Time-Life International, Seymour, 1964, p.79.
19 Bristowe, *op. cit.*, p.63, fig.29.
20 Richard South, *The Moths of the British Isles*, Series 1, Warne, London, 1961, pl.16.
21 V.J. Stanek, *The Pictorial Encyclopedia of Insects*, Hamlyn, London, 1969, p.412, fig.731, p.413, figs. 732, 733.
22 Jacques-Yves Cousteau and Philippe Diole, *Life and Death in a Coral Sea*, Cassell, London, 1971, p.290.
23 Walt Disney, *Wonders of the Ocean*, W.D. Productions, Amsterdam, 1967, p.40.
24 J.W. Steward, *The Snakes of Europe*, David & Charles, Newton Abbot, 1971, p.53.
25 *Ibid.*, p.126.
26 Morris and Morris, *op.cit.*, p.181.
27 *Ibid.*, p.173.
28 Steward, *op. cit.*, p.32.
29 *Ibid.*, p.34.
30 Lawrence Blair, *Rhythms of Vision*, Croom Helm, London, 1975 fig.29.
31 S. Peter Dance, *Seashells*, Hamlyn, London, 1971, p.69, ill.2.
32 *Ibid.*, p.71, ill.3.
33 *Ibid.*, p.69.
34 Ian Cox (ed.), *The Scallop*, Shell Transport & Trading Co., London, 1957, p.35.
35 Eugène N. Marais, *The Soul of the White Ant*, Penguin Books, Harmondsworth, 1973, pp.145-7.
36 *Ibid.*, pp.151-2.
37 *Koran*, trans. George Sale, Warne, London and New York, n.d., p.54, n.2.
38 *Ibid.*, p.54.

Chapter 3 Architectural sanctuary

1   C.G. Jung, *Psychology and Alchemy*, Routledge & Kegan Paul, London, 1968, revd edn, Collected Works, vol.12, p.220.
2   *Ibid.*, p.221
3   S. Peter Dance, *Seashells*, Hamlyn, London, 1977, pp.90-1.
4   Sir Cyril Fox, *Life and Death in the Bronze Age*, Routledge & Kegan Paul, London, 1959, p.171.
5   *Ibid.*, p.178.
6   Margaret A. Murray, *The Splendour That Was Egypt*, Sidgwick & Jackson, London, 1964, p.115.
7   R.J.C. Atkinson, *Stonehenge and Avebury*, HMSO, London, 1959, p.17.
8   *Ibid.*, p.11.
9   Amos Rapoport, 'The Pueblo and the Hogan', in Paul Oliver (ed.), *Shelter and Society: New Studies in Vernacular Architecture*, Barrie & Jenkins, London, 1971, pp.73-4
10   Barrie Biermann, 'INDLU: The domed dwelling of the Zulu', in Paul Oliver (ed.), *Shelter in Africa*, Barrie & Jenkins, London, 1970, p.101.
11   *Ibid.*, pp.101-2.
12   Sir Banister Fletcher, *A History of Architecture by the Comparative Method*, Athlone Press, University of London, 1961, p.195D.
13   *Ibid.*, p.31B.
14   *Ibid.*, p.122J.
15   *Ibid.*, p.122K.
16   *Ibid.*, pp.123, 124B.
17   Georges Lakhovsky, *The Secret of Life: Cosmic Rays and Radiations of Living Beings*, trans. M. Clement, Heinemann, London, 1939, translator's introduction, p.29.
18   Fletcher, *op. cit.*, p.24.
19   *Ibid.*, p.28.
20   *Ibid.*, p.32B.
21   Donald Robertson, *Pre-Columbian Architecture*, Studio Vista, London, 1968, fig.60.
22   *Op.cit.*, pp.128-9.
23   *Ibid.*, p.218.
24   Philip Rawson, *The Art of South-East Asia*, Thames & Hudson, London, 1967, p.55.
25   Graham Clark and Stuart Piggott, *Prehistoric Societies*, Hutchinson, London, 1965, p.275.

Chapter 4 Chemical secrets of ceremony

1 Ramona Morris and Desmond Morris, *Men and Snakes*, Hutchinson, London, 1965, p.23.
2 *Ibid.*, p.22.
3 See Sir John Marshall, *Mohenjo-Daro and the Indus Civilization*, Arthur Probsthain, London, 1931, vol.3, pl.CXVIII.
4 Experiment with a stuffed, well-grown male Impala in a museum showed that the extensive suppression of the spiral-and-curve horn shields extended to 71 cm across the creature's forehead and 79 cm from the forehead backwards along its body's sides.
5 Émile Durkheim, *The Elementary Forms of Religious Life*, Allen & Unwin, London, 1915, p.86.
6 *Ibid.*, pp.120-1.
7 Claude Levi-Strauss, *The Savage Mind*, Weidenfeld & Nicolson, London, 1966, p.239.
8 Graham Clark, *The Stone Age Hunters*, Thames & Hudson, London, 1967, p.103.
9 Durkheim, *op. cit.*, p.124.
10 *Ibid.*, pp.188-90.
11 Sir Leonard Woolley, *Excavations at Ur*, Ernest Benn, Tonbridge, 1954, p.64.
12 Juan Kelly, *The Manx Dictionary*, Douglas, Isle of Man, 1846.
13 E.O. James, *The Cult of the Mother Goddess*, Thames & Hudson, London, 1959, pp.46, 96–7.
14 *Ibid.*, p.96.
15 C.G. Jung, *Symbols of Transformation*, Routledge & Kegan Paul, London, 1956, Collected Works, vol.5, p.75, pl.XIIIa.
16 E.V. Hanauer, *Dolls of the Indians*, Thomas Yoseloff, London, 1970.
17 Georges Posener, *A Dictonary of Egyptian Civilization*, Methuen, London, 1962, pp.141-2.
18 O. La Farge, *A Pictorial History of the American Indian*, André Deutsch, London, 1958, p.28.
19 C.G. Jung, *Psychology and Alchemy*, Routledge & Kegan Paul, London, 1968, revd edn, Collected Works, vol.12, p.111. fig.53.
20 *Ibid.*, p.206.
21 *Encyclopedia Britannica*, Quarantine, from Italian 'quaranta' — forty was the number of days restricting travellers' movements during the bubonic plague.
22 S. Peter Dance, *Seashells*, Hamlyn, London, 1971, p.113, fig.5.
23 Litz Pisk, 'A Step in Time', BBC TV, *Omnibus*, May 1970. I am grateful to Litz Pisk for the ground plan of the Paesont-Braule.

24   Joan Lawson, *European Folk Dance*, Pitman, London, 1935, p.5.
25   If the traditional octomorphic date, 8 May, falls on a Saturday or Sunday, a shift of date is now made in deference to modern customs.
26   Woolley, *op.cit.*, pl.10b, Grave PG/1237.

Chapter 5   Radiational after-life

1   M. Murray, *The Genesis of Religion*, Routledge & Kegan Paul, London, 1963, pp.47-56.
2   J.E.Cirlot, *A Dictionary of Symbols*, Routledge & Kegan Paul, London, 1962, p.xx.
3   *Ibid.*, p.xxxii.
4   C.G. Jung, *Psychology and Alchemy*, Routledge & Kegan Paul, London, 1968, revd edn, Collected Works, vol.12, p.19.
5   *The Victoria History of the Counties of England, Cornwall*. vol.1, pl.XIX, fig.10.
6   D. McKenzie, *The Migration of Symbols*, Kegan Paul, Trench Trubner & Co., New York, 1926, pl.XIII, p.5.
7   *Ibid.*, p.152.
8   *Ibid.*
9   C. Desroches-Noblecourt, *Tutankhamen*, Penguin Books & George Rainbird Ltd, London, 1971, pl.XXX.
10   *Historical Relics Unearthed in New China*, Foreign Languages Press, Peking, 1972.
11   *Op. cit.*, p.95.
12   O. La Farge, *A Pictorial History of the American Indian*, André Deutsch, London, 1958, p.121.
13   BBC television programme, *Gilding the Lily*, 1974.

Index

Index